W9-DET-724

J 989.2 JER
Jermyn, Leslie
Cultures of the world Paraguay

Vail Public Library
292 West Meadow Drive
Vail, CO 81657

CULTURES OF THE WORLD

PARAGUAY

Leslie Jermyn

MARSHALL CAVENDISH
New York • London • Sydney

PUBLIC LIBRARY

Reference edition reprinted 2000 by
Marshall Cavendish Corporation
99 White Plains Road
Tarrytown
New York 10591

© Times Media Private Limited 2000

Originated and designed by
Times Books International, an imprint of
Times Media Private Limited, a member of the
Times Publishing Group

All rights reserved. No part of this book may be reproduced or
utilized in any form or by any means electronic or mechanical,
including photocopying, recording, or by an information storage
and retrieval system, without permission from the copyright
owner.

Printed in Malaysia

Library of Congress Cataloging-in-Publication Data:

Jermyn, Leslie.
    Paraguay / Leslie Jermyn.
      p. cm.—(Cultures of the World)
    Includes bibliographical references and index.
    Summary: Describes the geography, history, government,
economy, people, lifestyle, religion, language, arts, leisure,
festivals, and food of Paraguay.
    ISBN 0-7614-0979-3 (lib. bdg.)
    1. Paraguay—Juvenile literature. [1. Paraguay.] I. Title.
II. Series.
F2668.5.J47 2000
989.2—dc21   99–27257
               CIP
               AC

INTRODUCTION

PARAGUAY, IN THE HEART of the South American continent, has long been isolated from the world due to its geographic position and social conditions. Southeast Paraguay is a land of forests and rivers, while the northwest is one of the more forbidding regions for human habitation in the Americas.

Paraguayans are unique in that their modern culture is a true blend of European and indigenous ones. Theirs is the only country in the New World to have a native Indian language as an official language. Sadly, they have long been one of the most poverty-stricken populations in the Western Hemisphere. Paraguay has been governed by dictators since it became an independent nation. This has often meant that the country has been sealed off from the rest of the world or shunned by it. In 1989, the painful process of establishing a workable economy and democracy was begun. It remains to be seen whether poverty and a long history of undemocratic governments will be put behind them as they enter the next millennium.

CONTENTS

In Itauguá, a town in southern Paraguay, people make a special lace called *ñandutí* ("nyan-DOO-tee").

CONTENTS

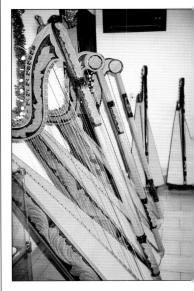

Paraguayan harps look much like European ones, but the sound they make is a little different.

GEOGRAPHY

THE REPUBLIC OF PARAGUAY is situated in the heart of South America. It is one of only two South American countries with no ocean coastline (the other is Bolivia). It has a surface area of 157,047 square miles (406,752 square km), which makes it approximately the size of California. The capital city is Asunción. Paraguay shares borders with Brazil in the east and northeast, Bolivia in the northwest, and Argentina from the southeast to the southwest. It is located between 19 degrees and 27 degrees, 36 minutes south latitude, and 54 degrees and 62 degrees, 38 minutes east longitude. The Tropic of Capricorn crosses the country at the town of Concepción.

Above: **The Paraguay River, with Asunción on the far bank.**

Opposite: **An aerial view of Asunción, Paraguay's political, economic, and cultural capital.**

There are three major rivers in Paraguay. The Paraná rises in Brazil and flows southward, defining the southeast and southern borders of Paraguay. The Paraguay, which gave the country its name, also has its headwaters in Brazil and flows south through Paraguay. The Pilcomayo starts in the Andes mountains and travels southeast, forming the border with Argentina. At Asunción, it joins the Paraguay, turns south, and continues to flow along the southwest border with Argentina.

The population is estimated to be 5.6 million, but it is not spread out evenly across the country. The Paraguay River forms a natural boundary between the two geographic regions of Paraguay: Eastern or Oriental Paraguay with its forests and gentle hills; and Occidental or Western Paraguay, otherwise known as the Chaco. Approximately 98% of Paraguayans live east of the Paraguay River, although this region only constitutes 40% of the land area. This curious concentration of population is easy to understand once you learn about the differences between the regions.

These regions offer striking contrasts: abundance of water in the east, little or no water in the west; luxuriant eastern forests, dry grasses and shadeless trees in the west; hills and meadows (east), flat prairie (west); lots of people in the east, almost no one in the west. They could almost be separate countries, but Paraguayans consider both sides of the Paraguay River to be complementary and equally important to their identity.

THE CHACO

Low Chaco marshes are filled with palms and water hyacinths.

Also known as "green hell," the Chaco Boreal (or simply the Chaco) is a broad plain with clayey and sandy soils. The Chaco is part of a larger area called Gran Chaco, which includes parts of northern Argentina and southern Bolivia. It has evolved over thousands of years from the dumping of silt by rivers flowing down from the Andes mountains in the west. Although the Chaco is almost uniformly flat, differences in rainfall produce areas of distinct vegetation: Low, Middle, and High Chaco.

In the Low Chaco, near the Paraguay River, the plains are under water most of the year due to flooding from the river and the soil does not absorb or drain water well. The landscape is dotted with marshes and ponds, caranday palms, and *monte* ("MOHN-tay"), a thorny scrub. As one moves northwest, conditions become more arid, with less ground water and rainfall. Much of this area is scrub with groves of trees that have incredibly hard wood, a result of growing slowly. Some people manage to live in the Low and Middle Chaco despite the harsh conditions, but cultivation is difficult, so most rely on cattle ranching. The High Chaco, near the Bolivian border, is dense scrub forest. Rainfall is unpredictable, and few live here.

There is a slight grade in the Chaco plain, with the north being higher than the south. South and east of the Paraguay River, the land is more habitable, and consequently the population is concentrated in the southeast.

EASTERN PARAGUAY

In contrast to the Chaco, travelers have characterized the eastern or Oriental region as "paradise on earth." There are plains, broad valleys, and forested plateaus. The highest peak—2,789 feet (850 m) above sea level—is in the San Rafael Cordillera in the southeast. Rainfall is more abundant and predictable in this region, making farming and forestry more productive. As well as being surrounded on the east, south, and west by large rivers, numerous smaller tributaries crisscross this region.

In eastern Paraguay, there are subregions characterized by different topography and vegetation. The most easterly portion is the Paraná Plateau, a forested area separated from the rest of eastern Paraguay by an escarpment. Around Asunción is the Central Hill Belt. This area is characterized by rolling hills with small isolated peaks and lakes. Its highest point is the city of Villarrica at 2,000 feet (610 m).

Between the plateau in the north and the Central Hill Belt in the south is the Central Lowland. Here, river valleys are broad and shallow and floods are common. Most of the lowland is a plain that gently rises to the plateau, but the landscape is dotted with thickly forested, flat-topped hills rising 20–30 feet (6–9 m) above the surrounding plain. These outcroppings cover anywhere from a few acres to a few miles and are known as *islas de monte* or mountain islands.

Finally, in southwest Paraguay is the Ñeem-bucú Plain. The Tebicuary River, a major tributary of the Paraguay River, bisects this flat region. Most of this area is swampy, but there are swells of higher land that remain dry and permit settlement. The eastern region is more amenable to human habitation because of its greater abundance of water and forest resources.

CLIMATE

Paraguay's climate is subtropical. The main determinants of the weather are the winds. In the summer months, October through March, warm, dust-laden winds blow in from the Amazon Basin in the north. In the winter, May through August, cold pampero winds from the Andes blow across the Argentine plain into Paraguay. With no natural wind barriers like mountain ranges along the way, the winds can develop speeds of 100 miles per hour (161 km/h) in southern Paraguay. Winds can also cause dramatic temperature changes in short periods of time.

There is no real spring or autumn in Paraguay, but April and September are transitional months between the two main seasons. Temperatures during these months are lower than the summer highs and may drop below freezing on occasion. Around Asunción, winter temperatures average 65°F (18°C) while summer sees averages of 75°F (24°C). In January, the hottest summer month, the daily average temperature is 84°F (29°C), and highs of 100°F (38°C) are common. It is much warmer in the Chaco, with highs over 100°F (38°C) quite normal in the summer.

Rainfall varies dramatically across the country. In the far eastern forest belt, average rainfall is 67 inches (170 cm) per year; in the far western Chaco, it averages 20 inches (50 cm) per year. The problem with rainfall in the Chaco is not just the small quantity but the irregularity and the fact that rain evaporates very quickly in this arid environment. This contributes to the challenges of living in the region and limits the range of crops that can be grown. The average rainfall diminishes as you move east to west, with Asunción getting about 51 inches (130 cm) per year.

Above: **A cattle ranch in the Chaco under flood waters.**

Opposite: **Paraguarí province lies in the Central Hill Belt.**

Rainfall is evenly distributed all year except for August, the driest month, and March to May and October to November, which are wetter than average.

The *ceibo pentandra* has a thorny, swollen trunk and is native to tropical America. Because of its shape, it is locally called the bottle tree.

FLORA AND FAUNA

Paraguay is a veritable garden of useful and edible vegetation. There are around 500 species of hardwood deciduous trees that can be used for lumber. The national tree, the *lepacho* ("lay-PAH-choh"), produces straight-grained hardwood and has multicolored flowers. The *quebracho* ("kay-BRAH-choh") grows in the Chaco. Its wood is said to be stone-hard and is harvested for its tannin, a chemical used in leather processing. There are also eucalyptus, cedar, and ceiba trees. The most famous Paraguayan plant is the *yerba maté* ("YAYR-bah mah-TAY"), a relative of the holly family that grows wild in the eastern forests and is harvested to make *maté* ("mah-TAY") tea. There are coconut palms, caranday palms, and palmitos, which produce the "palm hearts" we eat. There is a wild pineapple, *caraguatá* ("kah-rah-gwah-TAH"), that may be the original for the modern plantation fruit. Orange trees grow wild as does Indian corn. In the Chaco are grasses, cacti, and a bush resembling mesquite.

Although the Chaco does not hold much interest for people, it is a wildlife haven. Jaguars, pumas, and ocelots hunt here—and there is lots to hunt. Among the larger mammals are peccaries, deer, giant anteaters, armadillos, tapirs, coatimundis, and capybaras. Reptiles include the deadly coral snake and the anaconda, a constrictor. The semiaquatic anaconda hangs from trees and waits for prey and can reach 30 feet (9 m) in length. Bird species are numerous. There are large ostrich-like rheas that stand about 5 feet (1.5 m) tall and tiny hummingbirds that fit in the palm of a child's hand. In between, one finds ducks, pheasants, quail, partridge, kingfishers, egrets, herons, and storks. The marshlands in the southwest of the Chaco are ideal for these species.

At least 238 fish species have been cataloged in Paraguay's rivers. Sport fishermen covet the dorado, which can weigh up to 40 pounds (18 kg). There are also catfish, *mandi* ("MAHN-dee"), *manguruy* ("mahn-GOO-rooy"), and *pacú* ("pah-KOO"). Two of the stranger fish are piranha and lungfish. The lungfish can survive low water levels by sealing itself in mud. The most eaten fish of Paraguay, the *surubí* ("soo-roo-BEE"), lives in the Paraguay and Paraná rivers, feeding on bottom-dwelling fish. It can grow up to 5 feet (1.5 m) long and weigh up to 110 pounds (50 kg). Two species of caiman (a type of alligator) are also found in these rivers.

Eastern Paraguay has many of the same animals as the Chaco, but due to the expansion of human habitation and over-hunting, they are restricted in numbers and usually found in the forests of the Paraná Plateau. There

Above: **The capybara, or carpincho, grows to 4.5 feet (1.3 m) long. It is the world's largest rodent.**

Below: **The collared peccary was believed to be extinct until its discovery in Paraguay in the 1970s.**

The word chaco *comes from a Quechua word meaning "abundance of wildlife." (The Quechua are an indigenous group living in the Andes of Bolivia and Peru.)*

WEIRD AND WONDERFUL ANIMALS

The puma or mountain lion is certainly not weird, but it is wonderful. This cat's range is among the largest of the land animals, stretching from northern Canada to southern Argentina. Pumas can live in mountains, forests, and on open grasslands. Their pale brown to gray coat camouflages them in a wide variety of settings. They can jump as high as 32 feet (10 m) and kill their prey by breaking its spinal cord. Paraguay's other big cat is the jaguar. Jaguars have spotted coats like their African cousins, the leopards. They live near water as their favorite prey is river reptiles. They can kill caimans and swat fish out of the water with a paw. Unlike most cats, jaguars swim. The jaguar— *yaguareté* ("yah-gwahr-ay-TAY") in Guaraní, the dominant native language in Paraguay—is the king of beasts in this region of the world and figures in many myths and legends.

The tapir is one of the oddest looking animals. When Paraguay was first discovered, reports reached Europe about an animal with the trunk of an elephant, the hooves of a horse, and the size and coloring of a cow. It was not until 1750 that the first accurate description was made. The tapir stands 4.5 feet (1.4 m) high and is up to 8 feet (2.5 m) long. The larger females can weigh up to 730 pounds (330 kg). Tapirs like to live near water and bathe daily. They also take mud baths to protect themselves from stinging insects. Tapirs live alone or in pairs and are favorite prey of pumas and jaguars. Another odd animal found in Paraguay is the giant anteater. It can grow up to 7 feet (2 m) long and weigh 100 pounds (45 kg)—a lot considering that it eats only ants and termites. Anteaters catch their dinner with long tongues coated with sticky saliva. Since they have no teeth, the insects are ground up in the stomach by strong muscles. It takes about 30,000 insects per day to feed one of these animals!

The piranha, the fish of movies and nightmares, live in the Paraguay and Paraná rivers and their tributaries. There are 20 species of piranha, but only four are carnivorous. All of them, however, have a mouth full of razor-sharp teeth. Their name derives from the Guaraní *pirá rahi* ("pee-RAH RAH-ee"), meaning "tooth fish." After years of intensive study of the meat-eating species, scientists have concluded that piranha attacks are unpredictable. One thing they do know is that the piranha is attracted by fresh blood, and once they go into a feeding frenzy, they can reduce a cow to a skeleton in 30 minutes. They can measure up to 16 inches (40 cm) long. They are the favorite prey of caimans. As illegal trade reduces the population of caimans, piranhas are increasing in number.

Many animals of Paraguay are endangered, but some efforts are being made to establish reserves to preserve their habitat.

are a few animals not found in the Chaco, particularly birds of the parrot and parakeet families. The *Amazona aestiva*, whose local name is *loro hablador* ("LOR-oh hah-blah-DOR") or talkative parrot, is green with red and blue wing feathers and has a blue and yellow head. It is about 14 inches (35 cm) long and has feet adapted to living on tree branches. Like other parrots, it can learn words and phrases when domesticated and can even imitate people's voices. In the wild, it mates for life. Unfortunately, this animal is hunted for its feathers and meat and is endangered.

THE CAPITAL AND OTHER CITIES

The full name of Paraguay's capital city is Nuestra Señora Santa María de la Asunción (Saint Mary, Our Lady of the Assumption), but most people know it only as "Asunción." It has always been the administrative and economic center of Paraguay because of its location at the meeting of the Paraguay and Pilcomayo rivers. The city is located strategically where the Paraguay River and surrounding hills form a natural fortress, a feature quite attractive to the first Spaniards who arrived in the early 1500s. Until quite recently, the only way to ship goods into or out of Paraguay was by the Paraguay River to the Atlantic via Buenos Aires in Argentina. This has made Asunción the only real city in Paraguay for most of its history.

Downtown Asunción resembles other modern cities in the multitude of shops and traffic jams.

Today, more than 20% of Paraguay's population lives in the city (about 1.2 million people) and a total of 38% in the surrounding region. Historically, Paraguay has been predominantly rural with about 55–70% of its population living in the countryside. However, the trend since the late 1960s has been toward urbanization.

Although Asunción is by far the biggest city, Ciudad del Este has grown enormously in this period from a small town to a center with over 150,000 people. There are two attractions in Ciudad del Este: the hydroelectric project just outside the city at Itaipú and the Friendship Bridge across the Paraná River to Foz in Brazil. Itaipú was started in 1972 and completed in 1991. Throughout this period, the lure of jobs attracted many poor rural dwellers. In addition, the road connection with Brazil has fostered a booming business in contraband goods flowing in both directions. Another hydroelectric project at Yacyretá, outside Encarnación, and a bridge connecting this city with Argentina have fueled growth there, too.

There are numerous smaller towns scattered across the eastern region, but since only 20% of Paraguay's roads are paved (mostly those connecting Asunción with Encarnación and Ciudad del Este), these towns retain a rural character.

Opposite: **A bridge across the Paraná River connects Encarnación with Posadas in Argentina.**

Left: **Vintage streetcars are still widely used in Asunción.**

ASUNCIÓN: MOTHER OF CITIES

Asunción was founded in 1537, which makes it the oldest Spanish capital in southern South America. It was founded by accident. The third Spanish expedition to Río de la Plata, led by Pedro de Mendoza, attempted to settle at Buenos Aires in 1536, but an Indian attack forced the settlers to flee up the Paraná River to Santa Fé. From there, one of the settlers was sent upriver to explore the area. When he failed to return, another expedition went upriver to look for him. On their way back, one of the crew, Juan de Salazar y Espinoza, stopped at the site of modern Asunción and founded a settlement. This happened in 1537, on August 15, which in the Catholic calendar is the Feast of the Assumption—Asunción in Spanish.

The grid plan of the city was laid out in the 19th century, and most of the government buildings were built at that time. Development has been very slow until quite recently. The city had only 14 blocks of paved road as late as 1940. Water and sewage systems were not installed until 1955, and there were no storm drains until the 1980s, which meant that during the rainy season, the streets turned into raging rivers. With the development boom of the 1970s, highrise buildings, hotels, and offices sprang up in this almost rural city. Many of Asunción's poorer residents were forced to move into slums on the outskirts of town, and many of the city's green plazas were replaced by new construction. Now, Asunción resembles other modern South American cities in terms of buildings if not in size.

From 1537 to 1617, Asunción was the center of Spanish activity for all of southern South America. Adventurers and settlers from Spain came here first before moving on. In this way, Asunción was the starting point for at least eight other important Spanish cities, including Buenos Aires, and was known as the "mother of cities." In 1617 Buenos Aires was separated from the Province of Paraguay and Asunción declined in importance to become a backwater of South American cities.

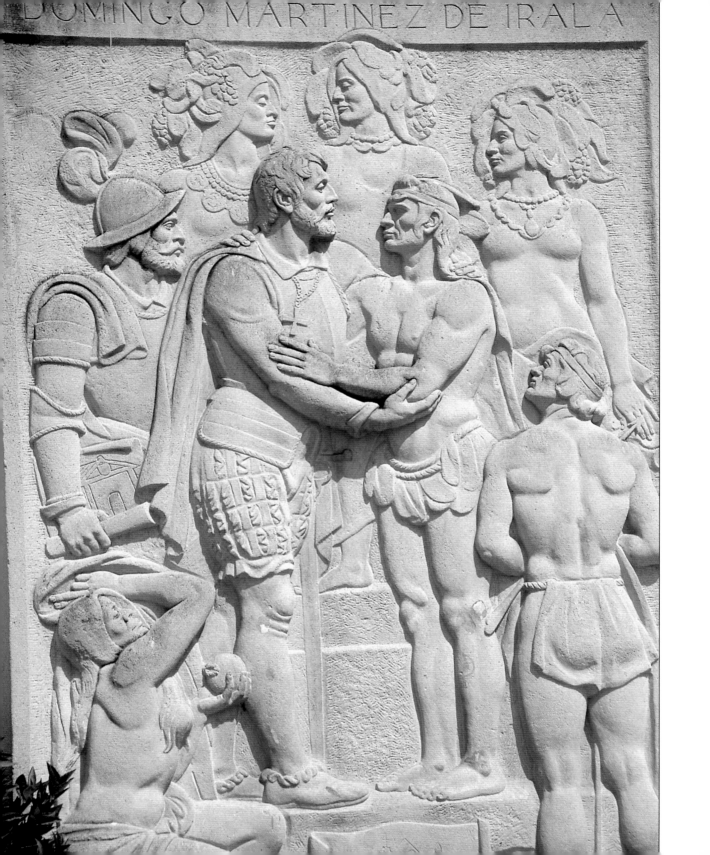

DOMINGO MARTINEZ DE IRALA

HISTORY

THE HISTORY OF PARAGUAY is quite tragic in some respects. There have been many dictators and a few disastrous wars. Despite these oppressive circumstances, Paraguayans have forged a distinct culture and national identity through the combination of both their native Guaraní and Spanish heritages. This chapter tells the story of how they did it.

BEFORE THE EUROPEAN CONQUEST

Paraguay was not "discovered" by the Europeans; people had already lived there for thousands of years. The major indigenous tribe occupied the eastern forest region. Today they are known as Guaraní, though when the Europeans arrived this group may have consisted of many subgroups that were known by different names. The Guaraní lived in small villages of 100–300 people. They combined farming in the forest with hunting, fishing, and gathering wild fruit and vegetables. Their main staples were corn and manioc (a root used to make flour). They also grew sweet potatoes, peanuts, pumpkins, bananas, papayas, and watermelons. To supplement this diet, they gathered wild foods such as honey and palm nuts and hunted tapirs and deer. They would also fish using wooden hooks or baskets.

A village would usually have four to eight large communal houses up to 165 feet (50 m) long. Everyone living in a house together was related through their male relatives. The men of a village would elect an informal chief, but much of the real power rested with the shamans (religious practitioners). Villages were seminomadic, meaning that when the fertility of the soil was exhausted after many years of planting, the whole village would move to a new area of the forest to farm fresh land.

Above: **The Guaraní practiced slash-and-burn farming: when it was time to clear new fields, the vegetation was first cut (slashed) and then burned to provide fertilizer for the soil.**

Opposite: **Spanish-Indian love and equality is the subject of this wall sculpture from the colonial period. It is found in the museum collection of the 19th century Cathedral in Asunción.**

Indians in traditional costumes: the village leader was selected from among the men, and men made the major decisions for their community.

In the Chaco, there were at least five different language groups. In this hostile environment, the indigenous people survived by combining a little farming with much hunting and the gathering of wild foods. They hunted deer, peccaries, tapir, and rheas, and in areas with rivers, they fished using nets. Women generally did the gathering of food, things such as edible cacti and water-lily roots. On their small farms, they grew corn, yucca, and beans. Chaco Indian groups lived in smaller villages and were also seminomadic to exploit resources in different areas. Their leaders were people who were very good at mediating conflicts and at persuading people to do things. These chiefs could not order people around, they could only ask or persuade gently.

Before the Spaniards arrived, there had been conflict among some of these groups. The Guaraní, in particular, had been expanding over the previous 2,000 years so that by the 1500s, they occupied a huge area covering much of the Amazon Basin and parts of Uruguay, Paraguay, and Argentina. This expansion was not always peaceful. Guaraní fought with local groups in order to take over their land. The Chaco groups closest to the Paraguay River periodically had to defend themselves from Guaraní invasions from across the river. This was the situation when the Europeans arrived.

THE FIRST EUROPEANS

The first European to see the land that would become Paraguay was Alejo García, a Portuguese explorer. García was shipwrecked off the coast of Brazil and learned to live with the Guaraní Indians of that area. From them, he learned of a mythical "white king" in the interior who had mountains of gold and silver. In 1524 he set off with a few Indians to explore the interior of the continent. He passed through eastern Paraguay where the local Guaraní volunteered 2,000 men to accompany him to fight the white king. This group crossed the Chaco and reached the edges of the Inca empire in Peru. There, they managed to steal quite a lot of gold and silver before the Inca chief chased them out. On his way back to the coast, García and his party were murdered by another group of indigenous people. For the next 30 years similar stories about precious metals would entice Europeans to come to Paraguay.

Asunción was settled in 1537 because it was a good site for a fort and the local Guaraní people were quite friendly. They welcomed the Spaniards with food and hospitality because they hoped these strange warriors would help them beat their enemies in the Chaco. Of course, the Spaniards were not interested in fighting Indians with no gold or silver, nor did they particularly want to settle at Asunción, they just wanted a camp from which to travel farther westward and the chance to find the rumored city of gold and silver. By the 1550s, enthusiasm for exploration was waning. The Spaniards had discovered that if they managed to cross the Chaco and the Andes, they simply found themselves in the new Spanish colony of Peru. They decided to settle the land as best they could.

The new settlers introduced *encomienda* ("ayn-coh-mee-AYN-dah"), a system designed to give each European rights to the labor and tribute of a number of Indians, in return for which they had his protection. In places like Mexico and Peru with large populations of Indians organized in complex farming societies, this system made some Spaniards very rich. In Paraguay, where the Indians had been hunters and gatherers and their populations were dispersed, there was little wealth to be taken or earned. Part of the problem was Paraguay's isolation from other colonies.

Spain had a very complicated system of trade in which all goods entering or leaving the New World had to pass through Panama. Goods destined for Asunción first had to be shipped across the Atlantic, carried overland to the Pacific side of Panama, shipped to Peru, carried overland to Buenos Aires (near the Atlantic coast), and only then taken upriver to Asunción. This meant, in effect, that trade was almost nonexistent, which had unfortunate consequences for the future of Paraguay.

In the 1600s descendants of the settlers realized they could grow two crops near Asunción: yerba maté and tobacco. Both crops were traded with Spain for goods not available locally. By this time, the children of the first Spanish-Guaraní marriages controlled the land and its wealth, such as it was. During the 1700s, they began to resent Spanish colonial power over trade and government. More Spaniards had arrived in Asunción in the 1700s, once they realized there was some money to be made in farming. There was friction between the two groups: the rural, Guaraní-speaking *mestizo* ("may-STEE-soh") elite and the Spanish-born and Spanish-speaking urban and government elite. In 1776 the affairs of Paraguay were put formally under the control of Buenos Aires, 1,000 miles (1,609 km) away. At the same time, the Spanish king increased taxes on Paraguayan exports, and this threatened to make trade impossible for them. It was the beginning of the end for Spain's control over its most isolated colony.

Gathering and curing yerba maté on the banks of the Paraná River. Yerba maté is a plant whose leaves are used to make a bitter tea containing caffeine and so has some of the properties of coffee.

SPANISH-GUARANÍ INTERMARRIAGE

Two conditions in Paraguay changed the face of the nation permanently: the nature of the social structure of the native population and isolation from Spain. The Guaraní were not well-administered. They lived in small, nomadic groups that foraged in the jungle. The only "government" the Guaraní had was an informal chief for each group.

When the Spaniards arrived to "govern" them, they found it very difficult to organize the Guaraní. If Asunción had been better connected with the other population settlements in South America, the Spaniards might have persevered in trying to change the Indians' way of life. But being far from their countrymen and having no wealth to trade or travel, they decided instead to adapt to the life of the Indians. Each Spaniard given a group of Indians under the *encomienda* system chose to live among them as their kinsman, taking over the position of chief. The Spaniards also accepted the Guaraní offer of wives; each settler had up to 20 wives. This meant, in turn, that lots of mestizo (mixed-race) children were born.

After only one generation, the rulers of the encomiendas were these mestizo children. By the 1700s, mestizos outnumbered Indians. Interestingly, these mestizos grew up speaking Guaraní, not Spanish, since their mothers and the majority of the population were Guaraní-speaking. This is the basis for the modern population of Paraguay.

INDEPENDENCE

The story of how Paraguay became the very first independent nation in all of South America is quite confusing. It all started in Europe when Napoleon took over the Spanish crown in 1808. Settlers in the New World loyal to Spain did not accept French rule. Consequently, in 1810, the local government of Buenos Aires expelled the French representative of the crown, claiming it would protect Spain's interests until a legitimate Spanish king sat on the throne again.

The leaders in Buenos Aires decided they would try to bring many other colonies under their control, by force if necessary. The mestizos of Paraguay had no intention of taking orders from Buenos Aires, however, once Buenos Aires no longer represented the Spanish king. An army from Buenos Aires arrived from down river in 1810, and mestizos and Spaniards fought together to resist it.

The mestizos and the Spaniards of Paraguay joined forces to fight the army from Buenos Aires, but they fought for different reasons. The Spaniards believed (incorrectly) that Buenos Aires was fighting to free the colonies from all control by Europe. The mestizos, on the other hand, had in the past resented control from Spain through Buenos Aires. They had welcomed their freedom from this control when France took over the Spanish crown; they had no intention of going back to the status quo.

The Spaniards left the battlefield the minute things looked bad. Despite this, the mestizos managed to repel the army from Buenos Aires. When the Spanish governor returned to assume command of the mestizos, he found that they despised and ridiculed him as a coward. He tried to disband and disarm them, but could no longer command their obedience.

In 1811 a Portuguese army lieutenant visited the governor in Asunción. The mestizos thought he was there to offer Portuguese Brazil's support to the Spaniards. (He was not, but rumors can be very powerful.) Having long considered the Portuguese their enemy, the mestizos perceived this visit as an act of treason. On May 17, 1811, they declared Paraguay independent of Spain.

A painting of Dr. José Gaspar Rodríguez de Francia, Paraguay's first president, who served from 1814 to 1840. He was born of European parents in the New World and was very well educated by Paraguayan standards.

A HERITAGE OF DICTATORS

For a few years following this declaration of independence, Paraguayans were quite paranoid that forces from either Buenos Aires or Brazil would try to take over their new country. From among the first five men appointed to rule the country, one man stood out as Paraguay's hope in avoiding invasion—José Gaspar Rodríguez de Francia. He negotiated an agreement with the leaders in Buenos Aires to leave Paraguay alone. Most Paraguayans were uneducated mestizo farmers; they were overly impressed with Francia's skills and knowledge. He convinced them, along with the urban elite, that he was indispensable. Anyone who was not convinced was killed or jailed by Francia's supporters. He was elected to the post of Supreme Dictator of Paraguay in 1814, and in 1816 a meeting of citizens declared him Dictator for Life.

Francia's tenure was one of mixed blessings for Paraguay. He closed the borders in 1818, forbidding anyone from entering or leaving. He overtaxed the urban elite and confiscated the land of the rural elite. The average farmer gained by these measures as land was leased to them very cheaply and surplus state-owned livestock was given away free. On the negative side, Francia spent almost no money on education or public works and forbade free speech or democracy in any form. He knew his enemies were likely to be other educated Europeans, so he terrorized them with torture and repression. He even made it illegal for European-born people to marry each other. They had to marry mestizos, mulattos (half black, half white), or Indians. This was to ensure they mixed with groups that were more supportive of him and did not form a tightknit group among themselves. Francia died in 1840, and though he was often cruel and despotic, he was honest. He never drew his salary nor did he tamper with the property and riches he took for the state.

In the year following Francia's death, there was chaos in Paraguay. Finally, in 1841 another Dictator for Life was named—Francia's nephew, Carlos Antonio López. He released Francia's 600 political prisoners but still forbade free speech. López was not as honest with public money, but he did spend some of it to build rural roads and 400 elementary schools. He also financed many new industries in Asunción, including textile production, arms manufacture, and a railroad. Paraguay was almost progressive under López. When he died in 1862, a congress of citizens elected his son, Francisco Solano López, as the new ruler.

Carlos Antonio López, Paraguay's second Dictator for Life, served from 1841 until 1862.

English settlers established rail travel in 1861. Today, wood-burning trains still run from Asunción to Lake Ypacaraí.

Was Solano López a megalomaniac or a man of courage in taking on the two biggest nations in South America? Whatever the truth, his country paid a high price in lost territory, lives, and resources.

The second López was less gifted than his father in foreign affairs. A policy of neutrality had been Paraguay's protection from invasion by larger powers. Solano López built up the army and tried to get Uruguay to form an alliance with him against Brazil and Argentina. These two nations had much bigger armies and Uruguay declined to fight them. In 1864 Solano López declared war on Brazil, and so began the War of the Triple Alliance.

WAR OF THE TRIPLE ALLIANCE (1864–70)

When the war began, it was between Paraguay and Brazil. Solano López sought permission to move troops through Argentine territory. When his request was denied, he did so anyway, and this provoked Argentina to join the war. Uruguay was forced to join the alliance of Argentina and Brazil.

Paraguayan soldiers fought bravely for six years, but their beleaguered forces had little chance of victory. After three years of fighting, 60,000 Paraguayan soldiers were dead. Another 60,000 were conscripted, including children less than 14 years old, slaves, and old men. Meanwhile, women worked for the war effort behind the scenes. Many soldiers had no guns and the cavalry was short of horses. The triple alliance occupied Asunción by 1869 and by 1870 Solano López was killed at the battle of Cerro Corá.

TRIPLE EFFECTS This war did not claim anywhere near the millions killed in the two world wars of the 20th century, but the impact on Paraguay in the 19th century was horrendous. The war's effects were felt in three areas: population, economy, and territory.

When the war began, Paraguay had 525,000 people with a roughly equal proportion of men and women. Six years later, only 221,079 people were left. Of the survivors, 106,254 were adult women, another 86,079 were children, and only 28,746 were adult men. It would take Paraguay generations to recover a normal population distribution. The second major effect of the war was economic. The victors imposed a huge fine on Paraguay to help pay for the costs of the war. This is standard practice when a country loses a war it started, but this debt was too big for a poor country with few able-bodied workers. Eventually, the government had to sell many of the country's assets to pay its debts, and this in turn affected the future of all Paraguayans into the 20th century. The third result of the war was that Paraguay was forced to give up territory to the two main victorious nations, Brazil and Argentina. Argentina took productive land in the southeast, while Brazil took land in the northeast. Paraguay lost Iguazú Falls, one of the world's natural wonders. In total, 55,000 square miles (142,450 square km) of territory was lost!

In the Panteón de los Héroes, built in 1863, lie the remains of Paraguayan heroes and leaders. Among them are Francisco Solano López, whose death ended the War of the Triple Alliance.

27

IN BETWEEN DICTATORS (1870–1954)

The victorious forces occupied Asunción and controlled the government for six years. One of their first acts as governors was to create the first constitution in Paraguay's history. Based on United States and Argentinean constitutions, it called for democracy and a separation of powers. For a country that had only seen government by dictators, this was too foreign a model. The 1870 constitution meant little in Paraguay.

With the new political system, two groups emerged: the Blues or Grand Club and the Reds or Club of the People. They later became the Liberal Party and the Colorado Party respectively. The Colorados were former supporters of López, while the Liberals had collaborated with the enemy. These parties were not based on ideas but on personal loyalties. Each group struggled to get their members into power in order to control state resources. The Colorados held on to power until 1904 when the Liberals started a rebellion. The Liberals' victory initiated 32 years of Liberal governments. This period of Paraguayan history was totally chaotic: there were 22 separate administrations (only one of them was Colorado), and a 14-month civil war that began in 1922. The Colorados had ruled with military strongmen during the 19th and early 20th centuries, and the Liberals continued this trend, only exchanging military generals for rich businessmen. At no time was there anything like democracy, and the common people were virtually ignored by the government.

The Liberals might have continued in power indefinitely but they made serious errors in dealing with Bolivia. Bolivia expanded its control of the Chaco in the late 1920s when they found oil in their part of the Chaco and suspected that the Paraguayan Chaco also contained reserves. They believed that Paraguay's army was too disorganized and underfunded to defend the territory. By 1932, border hostilities made war inevitable.

For a quarter century, from 1876 to 1900, a series of self-interested presidents sold off huge amounts of Paraguay's territory to foreign concerns. They kept the profits for themselves and left very little money for the state to use for the people. By 1900, 79 people owned 50% of all the land in the country and important industries were controlled by Argentineans, the British, North Americans, the French, and Italians.

Soldiers traveling back from the Chaco war front. The war wounded 250,000 people and killed 60,000 Bolivians and 40,000 Paraguayans.

During the three-year Chaco War (1932–35), the Paraguayan army fought hard to push the Bolivians back and the horrible Chaco climate helped them. Most of the Bolivian army consisted of Indians who lived in Bolivia's cold mountain areas. They suffered in the heat and did not know how to find water in the Chaco desert. Both sides, however, suffered terrible losses. In 1935, exhausted, they signed a peace treaty. Paraguay got most of the Chaco area (there was no oil in it after all) and in return gave Bolivia access to the sea via the Paraguay River.

Many people were displeased with the way the Liberals had managed the war. They tried to appease the soldiers by giving them a pension, but it was too little, too late. On February 17, 1936, in what is called the February Revolution, the military took control. Although it held power for the next 18 years, politics in Paraguay looked pretty much the same as always: chaotic. Political infighting as well as disagreements with groups outside the government prevented stability. By 1946–47, the country was once again plunged into civil war. One army officer who distinguished himself in this skirmish was Alfredo Stroessner.

Paraguayan intellectuals criticized the government openly when Bolivia encroached on Paraguayan territory. Later, many of them served in the reserve militia.

Above: **Alfredo Stroessner's courage in the Chaco War earned him a place in politics. Once he became president, however, he was determined to hang on to power.**

Right: **General Andrés Rodríguez helped alter the constitution so that presidents elected after Stroessner could not be reelected for a consecutive term. This is meant to prevent the rise of dictators.**

STROESSNER YEARS (1954–89)

By 1954, Stroessner was one of the few individuals in Paraguay to effectively hold power. When the president of the time tried to curb his influence, he forcibly took office. No one knew it then, but Paraguay had returned once more to a long-term dictatorship. Like his predecessors in the 19th century, Stroessner held power by exiling or killing his opponents. Unlike his predecessors, he held elections, thus observing the requirements of constitutional amendments he instituted in 1967. This document called for a bicameral legislature with two-thirds of the seats held by the political party that won elections and the rest divided among the opposition. Stroessner campaigned like any other politician, but with his absolute control of the army and support from wealthy Paraguayans, he never lost an election. The congress was always filled with his Colorado supporters, who rubber-stamped whatever he decided.

Opposition to Stroessner's virtual dictatorship mounted in the 1970s both internally and internationally. The Catholic Church and Amnesty International criticized his abuse of human rights, particularly of the rights of Indians. US President Jimmy Carter also criticized the regime, demanding changes. Stroessner gave in a little by releasing some political prisoners.

After a period of economic success in the late 1970s, Paraguay suffered a recession. By then Stroessner had run out of resources to exchange for support and was forced to borrow money from abroad. By 1985, governing was becoming more difficult, and Stroessner's health was failing. He still ran for leadership of the Colorado Party in 1987 and won. In 1989, however, one of his supporters, General Andrés Rodríguez, decided enough was enough. He tried to arrest Stroessner in his home; after a gunfight between his troops and Stroessner's personal guard, Stroessner surrendered.

AFTER STROESSNER

General Rodríguez started the process of creating democratic institutions. On June 18, 1992, a new constitution was approved that prevents anyone from having absolute control of the country.

On May 9, 1993, Colorado candidate Juan Carlos Wasmosy was elected with 39% of the vote. While Wasmosy was in office there were accusations of corruption and concern that the military would return. However, he maintained government control until elections were held in May 1998. The Colorado candidate Raúl Alberto Cubas Grau won.

Cubas Grau was not long in office. When his vice-president was assassinated in March 1999, he resigned amid civil unrest in the capital city, and went into exile in Brazil. Senate leader Luis Gonzalez Macchi became president.

International critics thought General Andrés Rodríguez was just pretending to change the system and had really just taken over from Stroessner. He had been Stroessner's second-in-command and had become very rich during his friend's years as president. He proved them wrong in 1993 by calling for elections.

GOVERNMENT

WITH THE RECENT RETURN to democracy, the government and political parties can operate as they were intended to under the constitution. In this chapter, we'll learn about the structures of government, political parties, and how Paraguayans choose their political leaders.

STRUCTURES OF GOVERNMENT

Paraguay's constitution, passed in 1992, is a remodeled version of that passed under Stroessner in 1967. Government power is centered in the executive branch—the office of the president and his cabinet. Paraguay is a republic headed by a president elected for a five-year term and assisted by a vice-president. The president appoints a 10-member cabinet to form the executive. He or she cannot be reelected for a consecutive term.

Below the president is a bicameral congress, which has an 80-member chamber of deputies and a 45-member senate. These representatives are elected at the same time as the president for the same duration. Citizens 18 years old and above are eligible to vote. The country is divided into 17 departments plus the capital city, Asunción. Each of these areas is administered by a governor, who is also elected every five years.

All judges are appointed by an eight-member Magistracy Council, an independent body that also appoints the electoral tribunal that oversees elections. The council is made up of elected members from the president's office (including the cabinet), congress, and the bar association (lawyers' group). The Supreme Court has nine judges. Justices of the peace deal with minor cases. The attorney general's office assigns officials to all judicial departments in the country.

Above: **The offices of the president and the foreign affairs ministry are in the presidential palace. The palace was planned for Solano López, but due to war and other problems, it was completed only in 1892, two decades after his death.**

Opposite: **Soldiers in dress uniform on guard at the Panteón de los Héroes.**

Most Paraguayans follow their family's traditional voting pattern regardless of who is running for election. Part of the reason for this is that the parties rarely espouse a clear philosophy. Being Colorado therefore means that one's family has always supported the personalities involved with the Colorados and will continue to do so.

The most important changes in the new constitution are ones that protect the people from dictatorial control: the president cannot hold office for two consecutive terms, and both houses of the legislature are elected by direct vote. Previously, the party with the most votes automatically got two-thirds of the seats in congress. Now, it may win the presidency but not have a clear majority in the house. Finally, the justice system has been fully separated from presidential control. An elected body, not the president, appoints members of the Supreme Court. This, too, serves to limit the power of any individual. Nevertheless, power is still concentrated in the center. Important decisions are made by the national government, not department governors.

POLITICAL PARTIES

The most powerful political party in recent years has been the Colorado Party (National Republican Association). This party was founded in 1880 and supported a strong state and military. It held power until 1904 and regained control of the government by supporting Stroessner's coup in 1954. Stroessner distributed favors through the party's huge network to guarantee its support during elections. After he was deposed, party affiliation no longer meant favors from the government, but many people remain loyal to the Colorados out of family tradition.

The Liberal Party was established in 1887 and formed a government in 1904 when it won a civil war against the Colorados. It supports laissez-faire economics, meaning it opposes state control of the economy. This policy did not work well after the Great Depression, and this, combined with the Liberal failure to direct the Chaco War, led to its downfall in 1936. The Liberals took over again briefly in 1939–40, but they have not returned to power since that time.

A COUNTRY OF CAUDILLOS

A *caudillo* ("cow-DEEL-yoh") is a "strongman"—someone who controls people's loyalty through a combination of threats and rewards. Most of Paraguay's leaders since independence have been caudillos, but three stand out for controlling the country for a long time—José Gaspar Rodríguez de Francia, Carlos Antonio López, and Alfredo Stroessner. They led the government for 85 of the years since independence in 1811. Why is Paraguay so vulnerable to dictatorial control? The answer has to do with its unique position in South America and its unique population.

From the beginning, Paraguay has been a backwater, stuck in the middle of the continent with no seaport and no mineral wealth. All three long-term dictators capitalized on this, and also kept relatively low profiles outside the country. If Paraguay were in Europe, these dictators could not have existed without far more international pressure being applied, especially in the 20th century.

If the Paraguayan people had always resisted dictatorship, the story might have been different. The bulk of Paraguay's population is politically quite conservative and not very wealthy. Moreover, education has never been a prime concern of the government. People did not formulate clear political agendas or demand that their government implement them. Politics in Paraguay was more a question of personal ties of loyalty and less of ideals: if someone you support gets into power, that means small favors for you, so the longer he stays in power, the better for you. This is true for people at all class levels. For a dictator to stay in control, he just has to keep giving favors to those who support him and get rid of those who don't. If he is clever, and the three caudillos mentioned above were clever, this game can be played for a long time before anyone gets too upset. The hope for the future is that under a stable democracy, people will get used to the idea of voting and choosing their future, thus blocking the path of potential caudillos.

The Febrerista Party (named after the February Revolution) was created in opposition to the Liberals in the 1930s. Its first leader was a Chaco War hero, Rafael Franco. Although it did not control the presidency for long, it passed the first labor code in Paraguay's history. It was formed by a mixed group of military personnel, intellectuals, and socialists. In 1947 Febrerista leaders were exiled and not allowed to return until 1967. By then, they commanded only 3% of the national vote.

Small, short-lived parties were created throughout the 20th century, and with the return to democracy there will be more. The two major parties will probably continue to govern for a long time. For the electorate, being Colorado or Liberal is like being Christian or Jewish—something you are born into. Paraguayans believe that party loyalty is very important and distrust people who switch allegiance or claim to be neutral. Here, more than in developed countries, democracy works through tradition.

President Juan Carlos Wasmosy (right) jokes with president-elect Raúl Cubas Grau on May 11, 1998, the day following the election. Cubas won with 55.4% of the vote.

CURRENT POLITICAL SITUATION

After Wasmosy was elected in 1993, his government did not run smoothly because his Colorado Party had not achieved a majority in either house. Opposition parties formed coalitions, and together with some dissatisfied Colorados, effectively blocked presidential initiatives. His attempts to get all factions to agree to govern together rather than block every initiative were stymied because there were so many controversial problems requiring immediate attention, which stirred up disagreement.

Some of the more pressing issues facing modern Paraguay include agricultural reform, workers' wages, military reform, and corruption in the government. Agriculture in Paraguay is outdated and underproductive. Large landowners have been allowed to leave their land undeveloped. Meanwhile, many small farmers lost their land in government takeovers and have nothing to farm. They demanded land reform to get back their land and better prices for agricultural produce. In the cities, workers demanded an increase in the minimum wage. When they threatened a general strike in 1995, the government finally capitulated and increased the minimum wage by 15%.

General Rodríguez had created a separate position of Commander of the Armed Forces. This person would no longer be the president as was customary, but a military man. The opposition parties wanted this law repealed. They believed that the president had to be commander-in-chief of the military in order to ensure its control by a democratically elected representative of the people. Wasmosy had to agree to this change in order to get cooperation in other areas.

RAÚL ALBERTO CUBAS GRAU Like Wasmosy before him, Cubas Grau is an engineer. He graduated in 1967 with a degree in electrical engineering from the Catholic University of Rio de Janeiro, Brazil. During the Stroessner years, he was involved in private business, eventually becoming director of a group of companies hired to repave the highway between Villarrica and Ñumi. He became involved in politics in 1994 when he was made executive secretary of the President's Social and Economic Planning Advisory Board. In 1996 Wasmosy made him minister of finance.

In 1998 he ran for president. Although he is a member of the Colorado Party, he represents a different faction of the party than Wasmosy. The 1998 election was reported to be fair and Cubas Grau won. He was inaugurated on August 15, 1998. Seven months later, however, he resigned following a controversy that arose when he freed General Lino Oviedo from 10 years' imprisonment. Cubas Grau's rivals in congress, led by Vice-President Luis Maria Argana, charged the president with abusing his powers and demanded Oviedo's rearrest. When Argana was assassinated on March 23, fighting escalated, causing the death of six people. The US Embassy in Asunción helped in negotiations that led to a transfer of power from Cubas Grau to Gonzalez Macchi.

The president's position in relation to the military is a sensitive issue in a country recovering from 50 years of military control. General Lino Oviedo was sentenced to 10 years in prison for engineering a military coup against Wasmosy in 1996. His release in 1998 led to civil unrest and the assassination of the Paraguayan vice-president in March 1999, the country's 10th anniversary of democracy.

ECONOMY

A COUNTRY'S HISTORY is often based on its economic resources and policies. Here, we'll learn about Paraguay's long-term dependence on agriculture, the significance of a single hydroelectric dam, and the economic crisis threatening the country.

BRIEF ECONOMIC HISTORY

As we learned in the previous chapter, Paraguay had no attractive resources for colonizers to plunder. For most of its early history, the country exported a few agricultural products like tobacco, yerba maté, and animal hides to Argentina. Under Francia (1814–40), the state controlled most of the land, which was leased out to small farmers, and prohibited foreigners from living in Paraguay. Antonio López (1844–62) allowed foreigners to enter the country and invest in business, but there was little to attract foreign investors. After the disastrous War of the Triple Alliance, economics in Paraguay changed. Successive governments had to cope with a huge war debt to Argentina and Brazil, which they tried to repay by selling Paraguay to foreign interests. This trend continued into the 20th century so that by 1935, a mere 19 companies owned half the economic wealth of the country.

By the time Stroessner came to power in 1954, he had to enforce stiff measures to control inflation and stabilize the currency. He depended on loans from countries like the United States to support his programs. Internally, because he had absolute control, he could force businessmen to accept his changes. He also took direct control of certain areas of the economy: railroads, shipping, meat processing, alcohol production, and telecommunications. He made it very attractive for foreign companies to

Above: **A farmer checks his yerba maté shrubs.**

Opposite: **Handpicking cotton, a major cash crop.**

The development of the Itaipú dam changed the country's economic landscape—from the growth of a boom town at Ciudad del Este to the creation of new jobs in construction and related industries.

do business in Paraguay. There were almost no taxes to be paid, and the regime was stable under Stroessner's iron hand. Throughout this period, the economy remained primarily agricultural, though this was slowly changing. In short, during Stroessner's early years, the economy grew very slowly, was primarily agricultural, and was dependent on large loans from foreign countries to make ends meet.

All this was to change in the 1970s when the Itaipú hydroelectric dam was built on the Paraná River in cooperation with Brazil. The project created jobs, and whole new sectors of the economy developed in construction and services for the workers. The promise of lucrative government contracts and cash wages attracted rich and poor alike to Itaipú, where a new city developed almost overnight at Ciudad del Este. At the same time, the government sponsored a land settlement program to promote farming in the eastern border regions. It offered parcels of state land at a low cost at a time when export crops like soybeans and cotton were in demand on the international market. Increased contact between Brazil and Paraguay over the Friendship Bridge (built near Ciudad del

ITAIPÚ: THE BIGGEST DAM IN THE WORLD

Itaipú is a dam across the Paraná River, which is the second biggest river in South America (the biggest is the Amazon). Paraguay and Brazil agreed to build the dam together. Because Paraguay did not have enough money to pay its half of the US$20 billion dollars that it cost, Brazil paid for Paraguay on the understanding that Paraguay would sell a lot of their share of the electricity to Brazil at a reduced rate.

Construction began in 1977 and employed 40,000 workers in round-the-clock shift work to build the dam as fast as possible. Whole new industries grew up to supply the workers with cement to build the dam. It is estimated that 141 million cubic feet (4 million cubic meters) of concrete was poured into this monster dam. When the river was dammed, it created a reservoir that extended 100 miles (161 km) upstream and flooded the large Guairá waterfall. The Itaipú hydroelectric plant produces 12.6 million kilowatts of energy every year. Itaipú is now the world's largest dam, surpassing even the Grand Coulee Dam in Washington State.

The construction of Itaipú created a boom in the Paraguayan economy. Although this boom is over, today there remains a whole new city called Ciudad del Este where there was once a construction site.

Paraguay's first source of hydroelectric power is the Acaray hydro-electric plant built in 1968. While the Itaipú dam was under construction, two other hydroelectric power projects were being negotiated with Argentina: the Yacyretá-Apipe and Corpus-Posadas projects.

Este) also promoted trade in contraband. Smuggling of cheaper Paraguayan goods to Brazil and Argentina and of stolen Brazilian goods into Paraguay has been going on for a long time, but bigger populations along the border made this even more attractive. All this rapid development attracted Paraguayan small farmers from the overcrowded area near Asunción as well as farmers from Brazil and as far away as Japan. Unfortunately, the boom years came to an end in 1982.

RECENT ECONOMIC HISTORY

Many factors combined to send Paraguay into crisis. The Itaipú boom was drawing to a close as the construction phase ended. World recession lowered prices of agricultural goods, and many countries reduced imports so that exporting countries sold less. Paraguay's foreign debt had reached critical proportions just when the country could least afford it. While the situation worsened, Stroessner had fewer resources to distribute to his political supporters and people began demanding change.

A blend of old and new transportation in the border town of Encarnación.

After the coup against Stroessner, General Rodríguez and President Wasmosy tried to undo some of the damage of the Stroessner era. Their strategy was to sell unprofitable state companies that had been created by Stroessner to give jobs to his friends. They also opened negotiations with other countries and foreign banks to restructure loan repayments and further economic cooperation. Finally, they reformed the tax system. Under the dictatorship, Stroessner was reluctant to tax potential supporters, but in a democratic system, Paraguay can tax personal income and business profits. This reform, however, has yet to be implemented.

ECONOMIC SECTORS

The agricultural sector is still the primary employer in Paraguay. About 40% of the labor force is engaged in farming, either for subsistence or export. Agriculture accounts for 24% of the total economic production. The main export crops are soybeans, cotton, sugarcane, corn, cassava, and wheat. Paraguay also exports wood and livestock such as cattle and pigs.

The next biggest employer is industry, which includes mining, manufacturing, construction, and energy. In total, about 27% of people work in industry. Mining is a very small component of the economy, though foreign oil companies are still exploring the Chaco region for petroleum deposits.

Manufacturing employs 11% of workers, and most factories process agricultural products. Some examples are food processing plants to convert raw food into packaged, cooked food; cigarette companies; textile factories to process wool and cotton into cloth and clothing; paper and printing factories; and leather factories to make hides into usable products like jackets. Construction is quite important and employs 10% of workers.

At a tile factory near Encarnación. Throughout Paraguay, wood is still widely used as fuel.

The primary source of energy is hydroelectric. With so many big rivers, Paraguay is an ideal place for this type of energy production. Once built, hydroelectric plants do not need many people to operate them. Paraguay now produces more electricity than it needs and sells the excess to Brazil and Argentina.

The service sector is comparatively small, employing only about 15% of the working population. This sector includes transportation, communication, restaurants, hotels, real estate, and financial services such as banking. There is an average unemployment rate of 10% while the balance of workers are employed in areas not measured by the government when compiling economic data. One of the main informal or uncounted industries is smuggling.

Ciudad del Este is a hive of shopping activity. Cheap Paraguayan goods are bought in quantity and smuggled across the border to Brazil.

Stroessner, who encouraged smuggling, used to say that "contraband is the price of peace." What he meant was that allowing people to make money illegally kept them happy and therefore peaceful.

TRADE

Trade is a vital source of government revenue through the collection of taxes imposed on imports. Paraguay's main trading partners are Brazil, Argentina, Uruguay, the United States, and Japan. Paraguay's main exports are agricultural products such as soybeans and cotton and processed products such as cloth and wood products. Its main imports are machinery, cars, petroleum products, household appliances, and beverages.

One problem that has plagued trade relations between Paraguay, the United States, Argentina, and Brazil is smuggling. This is where people bring goods across the border without declaring them to the authorities and hence without paying taxes on them. Under Stroessner, this was encouraged. Brazil, Argentina, and the United States have been urging Paraguay to control smuggling for a long time. The smuggling works this way: Paraguay has low taxes on imported goods such as alcohol, perfume, and cigarettes—much lower than its neighbors—so Argentineans and Brazilians regularly enter Paraguay to buy these goods to bring home.

Paraguayan smugglers also arrange to deliver these goods to cities such as Buenos Aires and São Paulo. They bribe the border official and drive truckloads of contraband across the border. In the other direction, stolen Brazilian cars, often violently taken from their owners, are the most popular illegal trade item entering Paraguay for resale. Finally, the United States has been concerned about Paraguay's involvement in drug smuggling. Cocaine is not made in Paraguay, but drugs enter and leave the country without much interference. Drug smugglers, the richest members of civilian and military groups, arrange to have drugs flown or driven in from Bolivia, then sent out again on flights of the national carrier, Paraguayan Airlines. With the military no longer in control of the government there is hope that Paraguay will cooperate in stopping this trade.

Loading and unloading at a harbor on the Paraguay River.

Rampant smuggling may eventually cease because Paraguay has joined a free trade alliance with Argentina, Brazil, and Uruguay called MERCOSUR. In this agreement, which came into effect in 1995, goods traded among these countries are not taxed as they pass across borders. Free trade agreements such as this are designed to help participating countries by expanding the market for their goods. The idea is that everyone can make what they do best, and then export to everyone else tax-free. In economic terms, it is like making one big country out of four smaller ones. This will certainly limit the smuggling of legal goods such as alcohol and small appliances since there is no longer an incentive to avoid taxes—the taxes are gone. There is still the problem of drug smuggling, but as Paraguay improves its formal or legal economy, there may be fewer people willing to take the risk of illegal trade.

Gauchos round up cattle using lassos. Estancias or ranches belonged to a very small proportion of the population, many of whom had amassed land during the dictatorial Stroessner regime.

WORKING LIFE

Agricultural laborers still make up the largest proportion of Paraguayan workers. In Paraguay's early history, there was more land than people to farm it. Various governments encouraged farmers from other countries to settle in Paraguay and work the land. As the rural population grew, education and access to government services were neglected. Most rural people were poor, but as long as there was land to grow their own food, they survived. Stroessner changed this dramatically.

In the last 20 years of Stroessner's rule he decided to develop large-scale farming, since only big farms efficiently produced enough cotton, cattle, or soybeans for export. A small farmer usually devoted most of his land to growing his own food and only a little to growing produce for sale. Such farmers made up the bulk of Paraguay's population. To reorganize the country for large-scale production, Stroessner expelled the peasants from their land and sold it to his wealthy friends for development.

By the 1990s, the rural situation was critical. Landless farmers started squatting on land to make a living. Many peasants moved into the cities in the hope of finding work. But when there was high unemployment in the cities, workers had no recourse to family farms that once provided sustenance. Until 1982, 57% of Paraguayans lived in the countryside; 10 years later the majority (51%) lived in cities. Heavy country-to-city migration places a great burden on the state. Often uneducated and untrained for urban work, peasants end up doing part-time or illegal work. This is a problem across Latin America but is especially so in Paraguay where the state has little money to help these people survive and too small an industrial sector to employ them. The answer lies in reform of land ownership in the countryside, but this is very difficult to do.

By 1981, as a result of Stroessner's land policy, the degree of concentration of land ownership was staggering: the top 1% of landowners owned 79% of the land, while the bottom 35% owned only 1% of the land. This 35% may even be considered lucky since another large group of people lost all their land and had to move to the cities for work.

Landless peasants swell the outskirts of the cities, often living in makeshift housing without water or sewers.

Paraguay, like all countries, has to start treating its land and the people who depend on it with respect if it is to have a stable economy and society.

LAND USE

The idea that land is inexhaustible has guided government programs since independence. Policies based on this erroneous assumption have brought Paraguay to a critical point. Similarly, the indigenous people, though a relatively small group, face social and economic crisis as a result of policies that have not heeded ecological issues.

Human use of the land can be divided as follows: the central zone around Asunción, the eastern zone farther from Asunción but still east of the Paraguay River, and the Chaco. The central zone has been settled for the longest time and has the highest population density. Some indigenous groups live in the eastern zone, which has recently been opened to settlement to relieve population pressure in the central zone. The Chaco, underpopulated for most of its history, has recently become a target for settlement and agricultural development (including forestry).

There are so many people in the central zone that the forests are nearly gone. In this region many farms are too small for people to make a living. This leads to methods of farming that deplete the soil: land is farmed every year without fertilizers, which are too costly, the soil becomes exhausted, and the crop yield diminishes. On bigger farms, owners are unconcerned about protecting the soil because they have so much of it. Again, the soil is worked to exhaustion.

Stroessner's government decided to relieve some of this pressure by opening land farther east for farming. Unfortunately, it did not enforce controls on how the land was used. To clear the land, settlers arriving from the central zone, whether small farmers or large, simply cut the forests at an alarming rate. Settlers also took land informally owned by indigenous peoples. There have even been government-sanctioned acts of violence against native people in order to take their land. The pattern of land

In Alto Paraná, the forested region in eastern Paraguay, trees are cut down for timber and firewood and to clear land for farming.

mismanagement in the central zone is being repeated in the east. The Chaco has been similarly exploited: forests are being harvested and farming is taking their place.

Paraguay depends on farming and forestry for a large proportion of its exports. By harvesting the forests without a policy of replacement, there will soon be no trees left to exploit. By not promoting better farming methods, the soil becomes depleted and yields decrease, and each year, the same piece of land produces less and less cotton or soybeans. It would actually be in the state's interests to help farmers protect the soil so that it produced the most crops possible every year.

Finally, Paraguay's Indians have been losing their land continually since the 1960s. Without land, they are forced to change the way they live and their culture. When this happens to people, they often lose their will to live and turn to self-abuse, using drugs and alcohol, or commiting suicide. The ecological crisis affects not only the soil or the number of trees; it is also a social problem.

PARAGUAYANS

PARAGUAYANS ARE UNIQUE among the other different peoples of South America. The majority are rural, poor, and of a single ethnic background. Some of this is changing with recent shifts in the economy and the addition of new ethnic groups from abroad. This chapter will cover these themes as well as introduce some important individuals from Paraguayan history.

ETHNIC GROUPS

MESTIZOS Paraguay is one of the most homogeneous countries in South America. Most people are of the same ethnicity—mestizo, or descendants of the first marriages between Spaniards and Guaraní during the early colonial period. About 95% of the modern population of Paraguay is made up of this group and their primary languages are Guaraní and Spanish.

There were few Spaniards in this part of the New World because of the absence of mineral wealth and large Indian societies whose labor could be exploited. Those Spaniards who settled the region married the local Guaraní and adapted to their way of living.

Left: **A Chulupi Indian community. There are 40,000 to 100,000 Indians belonging to 17 ethnic groups. Many of them live in areas not covered in the population census.**

Opposite: **Mestizo children in Itauguá, a town near Asunción.**

German immigrants with a mestizo friend. The inhospitable Chaco is the location of three major German Mennonite colonies—Fernheim, Menno, and Neuland.

AFRICANS The remaining 5% of the population is an interesting mixture of ethnic groups. They include some 10,000 people of African descent, whose ancestors were slaves brought to Paraguay beginning in colonial times. They were absorbed into the mestizo and Indian populations through intermarriage, and many of them are not easily distinguishable from the majority in appearance or language.

IMMIGRATION POLICY Other groups began arriving after the War of the Triple Alliance. More than half the total population was killed in that war, so successive governments wooed migrants from abroad to repopulate the country. Between 1882 and 1907, about 12,000 immigrants arrived in Asunción. Three-quarters were from Europe, mainly Italy, Germany, France, and Spain. The rest came from neighboring countries and from the Middle East. Most of them joined urban trades and commerce and became the core of the middle class.

JAPANESE In the 20th century, through joint agreements between Paraguay and Japan, Japanese farmers established agricultural colonies near Asunción and Encarnación. Today, they number about 8,000. The Japanese have learned to communicate in Spanish and Guaraní, but generally have not intermarried with mestizos.

MENNONITES Another group that has remained largely separate from the majority are the German-speaking Mennonites. They began to settle in the Chaco region in the 1920s and 1930s. The first Mennonite groups to arrive were from Canada; they emigrated because the Canadian government

tried to replace German with English as the language of instruction in their schools. Subsequent groups came from the Soviet Union in the 1940s, fleeing religious persecution there. Today, there are about 15,000 Mennonites living in Paraguay, with two-thirds settled in the Chaco region.

Gauchos of the Chaco region. Many indigenous people of this region were displaced when land was granted to settlers for cattle ranching.

KOREANS, CHINESE, BRAZILIANS The most recent immigrants arrived from Korea, China, and Brazil. Some 30,000 Koreans and Chinese came to Paraguay in the late 1970s to take advantage of the Itaipú boom years. Most live in Ciudad del Este and Asunción and are involved with trade in imported electronic goods from Asia. Attracted by low land prices near the eastern border, Brazilians arrived in even greater numbers: estimates vary from 100,000 to 350,000. There are enough of them living along the Paraguay-Brazil border that Portuguese is heard more than Spanish or Guaraní in that region.

INDIANS The final piece of the Paraguayan puzzle is filled by indigenous Indian groups of a variety of ethnicities. Again, numbers are not precise,

A Mennonite family clears brush from a dirt road in Neuland, a Mennonite community in the Chaco. Successive governments encouraged the settlement of the Chaco because they believed the undeveloped land could be put to agricultural use.

partly because relations between Indians and other Paraguayans have not usually been peaceful so the Indians resist being counted by the state, and partly because these groups are scattered throughout the country, often in the most remote areas. Somewhere between 1% and 2% of the population are Indian. They are believed to belong to 17 different ethnic groups, including Chulupi, Aché, Lengua, and Macá. Thirteen groups live in the Chaco and speak four different languages, while the four groups living in eastern Paraguay speak varieties of Guaraní. Their way of life has survived in the 20th century because they have tended to live far from the most settled region around Asunción.

The existence of indigenous people living in the eastern forests has been severely threatened since the government actively began promoting large and small-scale farming in the region. Since the Indians were using much of this land, they were forcibly removed when new settlers arrived.

The Chaco groups west of the Paraguay River were once even more isolated. But they were caught up in the Chaco War and often used as scouts by both the Bolivian and the Paraguayan armies. They also lost land to Mennonite settlers and large ranching concerns that invaded the region before and after the war. Since many of the Chaco Indians were primarily hunters and gatherers, they were negatively affected when ranchers started fencing off the land and prohibiting them from using it.

Sadly, despite the half-Indian heritage of the mestizo majority, they are quite racist toward Indians and have treated them cruelly in recent years. How this has happened is explained in this and the next chapter.

Some Indian women in Filadelfia, a town in the Mennonite colony of Fernheim, find employment in domestic service.

POPULATION FEATURES

Paraguay has been a predominantly rural country for a long time. Since the 1960s, however, there has been internal and external migration. Internally the pattern was more urbanization, with rural people moving into cities or larger towns. Overcrowding in the agricultural zone around Asunción is partly responsible. Peasants have been forced off their land by large landowners and have had to go to Asunción or farther afield to find employment. When the Itaipú project started, there was a construction boom all over the country and many rural poor were attracted to either Ciudad del Este in the east or to Asunción. Now, slightly more than half the population lives in urban areas.

Another general trend in internal migration has been toward the eastern border with Brazil. There were several reasons: the Itaipú project created jobs; convenient road access via the Friendship Bridge increased trade with Brazil; and the government sold land in the area at a low price. The two areas with the highest population density are Asunción and the

Good health services affect the population directly by increasing life expectancy and reducing infant mortality. When children are more likely to live to adulthood, people tend to have fewer children. For reasons given in the next chapter, the health system in Paraguay has not been able to make this happen.

surrounding countryside, with more than 100 people per square mile (40 per square km), and the eastern border region, with 40–100 people per square mile (15–40 people per square km). By comparison, the Chaco has fewer than five people per square mile (two people per square km).

While many rural Paraguayans have migrated to the cities, many others have left to find work in Argentina. This is an ongoing trend but one that has increased in modern times. Again, due to a lack of land in the central farming region, many men have been forced to seek work elsewhere. Many of them ended up in northeastern Argentina, on tobacco plantations or in the textile and lumber industries. Women also left, but mostly headed for Buenos Aires where they worked as maids. At the last reliable count (in the 1970s), there were between 470,000 and 600,000 Paraguayans living in Argentina. This is a huge number, representing nearly a quarter of Paraguay's population at that time.

Migrant workers tend to be young, contributing to the fact that Paraguay's population has aged slightly on average. It is still a predominantly youthful population, with 42% younger than 15 years. This is because life expectancy in Paraguay, at 67 years, is quite low, while at the same time the birth rate is quite high, about 4.6 children per woman. Since people do not live very long and many children are born, Paraguay has a young population that is growing in size.

SOCIAL CLASSES

Paraguay is different from its neighbors in one respect: while most Latin American countries have three distinct economic groups, Paraguay has predominantly a single class: poor. The Spanish colonial elite that survived into the post-independence period were killed in the War of the Triple Alliance. Those remaining were largely poor, rural, and mestizo. Since then, there has emerged a very small urban middle class: a few thousand people, mostly immigrants from Europe and Asia.

The ruling elite is a tightknit group of families living in Asunción that controls most industry, large-scale agriculture, the military, and politics. The people belonging to this small and exclusive group know each other and grew up together, attending the same schools. Unlike in other Latin American countries, this group is not of pure European descent, but is mestizo, just like the majority of poor peasants. Hence the large lower group and the tiny upper group are ethnically the same, while many of the middle class are ethnically different. This is unusual.

The lower social group has never been well organized to fight for rights. Political parties kept people loyal by handing out small favors and threatening those opposed to them. This is partly why the poor have not organized and challenged government policies that disadvantaged them. Also, nearly 100 years of dictatorship has conditioned people. For example, Stroessner forbade unions for industrial workers; since the return to civilian government, unions have started organizing for workers' rights, but the laws are not in their favor. It can take years to get government permission for a legal strike, so any that have occurred have been illegal and have faced police violence. In another example, the Roman Catholic Church tried to help peasants form groups to demand land redistribution. This, too, was unsuccessful; the authorities would not tolerate organized protest.

Social relations between the elite and the poor have been characterized by exploitation met with quiet acceptance. Poor living conditions are accepted with quiet resignation.

A Macá Indian in traditional clothes in the Macá colony. The colony was established in 1944 to save the Macá and their culture from extinction.

DRESS

Traditional dress, like so much else, reflects a history of largely rural settlement. Men wear full trousers of brown, light gray, or bright blue fabric and a loose shirt open at the neck. Bandanas are loosely tied around their necks, and they wear flat-topped, cowboy-style hats, sometimes decorated with red, white, and blue (national colors) flowers around the brim. To complete the outfit, there are leather boots, a striped poncho, and a wide cloth sash around the waist. Women's traditional dress is a full pleated skirt worn with a white apron that is often decorated with lace. Under the skirt and showing below its hem, they wear big ruffled petticoats of white cotton. Their blouses are worn off the shoulder and the sleeves are made of lace. The body of the blouse is often embroidered in red, white, and blue to match the men's hats. Their hair is worn up and they wear jewelry of silver or coral.

This type of dress is no longer seen in the countryside, though tourists can see examples of it at Folkloric Ballet performances. Most people wear mass-manufactured clothes made locally or imported. In the city, most people are dressed the way people are in any city anywhere in the Western world.

FAMOUS PARAGUAYANS

Stroessner: Strongman of Paraguay Alfredo Stroessner's father was a German immigrant and his mother a Paraguayan. At 16 he enrolled in the military academy in Asunción, and three years later he was sent to fight in the Chaco War. Twice decorated for bravery, by the end of the war he was a first lieutenant. In 1940, by then a major, he was selected for special training in Brazil. He returned to Paraguay to command his own artillery unit. He became involved in politics when he fought for the Colorado government in the 1947 civil war. The party made him commander-in-chief in 1951, thereby putting him in a position to seize power for himself in 1954.

His 35-year dictatorship was the longest in Latin American history. He managed to hold power for so long because he controlled the Colorado Party machine of favors and threats and had the respect of the military due to his war-time bravery. Unlike many dictators, Stroessner was not personable nor was he a great supporter of the common person's needs. He worked incredibly hard though, and no detail escaped him. By sheer dint of hard work, he controlled life at every level for most citizens. Had he turned the same energy to preserving democracy and individual rights, Paraguay would be in an enviable position today.

Godoi: Paraguay's First Patron of the Arts Juan Silvano Godoi was born in Paraguay in 1850. When the War of the Triple Alliance started, he was sent to Argentina to study law. He was then 15. Five years later he returned and was part of the group that wrote the constitution of 1870. Godoi was opposed to the Colorado Party. He joined a rebellion in 1877, and when it failed, he was exiled. Back in Buenos Aires, he became successful in business and his wealth funded another revolution in 1889. When this too failed, Godoi dedicated himself to writing about the Triple Alliance War and collecting books and works of art. He returned to Asunción in 1895, and generously created a public library and museum from his collection: the Godoi Museum in Asunción was the first museum created in Paraguay. When he died in 1926, the state took over the museum. Godoi also left behind personal papers and newspaper clippings from his time. The most valuable item in this collection is a 10-volume personal diary covering the period 1897–1921 and detailing many events in Paraguay's history. These papers, known as the Juan Silvano Godoi Collection, are in the United States, in the library of the University of California at Riverside.

Belaieff and the Macá Indians General Juan Belaieff of Russia fled the revolution there in 1917 to teach at the military college in Paraguay. He became the army's director of cartography and was the first to complete surveys of the Chaco region. During the Chaco War, he befriended an indigenous group called the Macá who helped him scout out the area. When war ended, Belaieff dedicated his life to understanding Macá culture and published scholarly works on the subject. In the 1940s, alarmed at the plight of Indians being forced off their land by ranchers in the Chaco, Belaieff convinced the government to donate land for a Macá reserve. The Father Bartholomew de las Casas Colony, on land held in trust by the Indigenous Association of Paraguay, was established in 1944 and attracted Macá who had been scattered around the Chaco. Today, it has a few hundred Indian residents.

LIFESTYLE

WE HAVE LOOKED AT Paraguayans in broad terms. Now we shall learn about family life, education, health, housing, and gender roles. As in many other countries, poverty often plays a key role in conditioning lifestyle.

MESTIZO HERITAGE

The Paraguayan lifestyle is a blend of traditions from Indian and European cultures. Spanish culture did not become dominant here, as it did in other Latin American countries, nor were native cultures all destroyed. In fact, the mestizos of Paraguay are as much products of their Guaraní great-great-great-grandmothers as they are of their Spanish great-great-great-grandfathers. The language of most homes is Guaraní, not Spanish, and many family traditions observed today are directly related to Guaraní social customs. The Spaniards did not so much conquer Paraguay as blend in with its largest cultural group, the Guaraní.

Above: **The single-horse covered wagon is commonly seen in rural parts of Paraguay.**

Opposite: **A farm worker and his family gather for a group picture outside their adobe and thatch house.**

RURAL VERSUS URBAN

Much will be made here of the differences between rural and urban Paraguay. These differences have become more marked in the second half of the 20th century, because until about 40 years ago, almost everyone lived in the countryside. Most of what we identify as particularly Paraguayan has its roots in their mestizo and rural past. These two facts of history have shaped modern culture more than anything else.

Before there was excessive competition for farmland, peasants (small farmers) moved around cultivating free land wherever they found it. Like their Guaraní ancestors, they used slash-and-burn cultivation. When yields decreased from soil exhaustion, the peasant would move to another area.

Village roads are well-traveled paths cleared of plants and leading to or past houses. Amenities such as electricity for street lamps do not exist, and on a moonless night, paths and everything outdoors are covered in total darkness.

Most people with small holdings did not have formal title to or ownership of their land. Since they were mostly nomadic, they did not bother applying for ownership, or they could not get it, even if they wanted to, because they were farming land belonging to a larger estate.

In the latter case, relations between the peasants and landowners were well defined, though actual rights to the land were not. The large landowner was known as *patrón* ("pah-TRONE"), while the peasant was called the *peón* ("pay-OHN"). Patrón-peón relations were set by custom rather than by law. The patrón allowed the peón to farm on his land in return for occasional gifts of produce on the patrón's birthday or at harvest time. Sometimes the patrón demanded labor from the peón. This was never done directly, but followed a pattern of etiquette. The patrón suggested that he needed a favor, the peón responded that he would be glad to help. Relations were never put into hard terms. There was no preset price in goods or labor, just customary relations of favors and gifts.

Beyond the economic sphere, patróns were also supposed to help peóns during crises. When a family member died, for instance, the patrón was expected to help with funeral costs. When the peón had trouble with the law, the patrón acted as his protector. In return, the peón owed the patrón loyalty. In politics, this meant that the peón was expected to support candidates the patrón favored. These ties lasted for generations. Interestingly, such long-term loyalty between poorer and wealthier people carried over into other realms. People often patronized only one storekeeper, even when the competition offered better prices. In return, storekeepers gave loyal customers special deals. Paraguayans still relate to one another in this way.

There were also customary relations between neighbors. They helped each other at harvest or planting time, and once again, the relationship was never formalized. No one paid a neighbor for his work, but they knew that they owed him a favor at some later date. This type of relationship cemented a community together.

Small villages scattered along the dirt roads linking farms were collections of essential services like the general store and the church. The commonest form of transportation in isolated regions was—and still is—the ox-drawn cart. With so few paved roads, cars and trucks were impractical. Local craftspeople, teachers, and government officials lived in town and a few peasants made a living as domestic servants for these people. Other than for festivals or essential commercial transactions, peasants did not come to town regularly. Larger landowners also maintained residences in town, and townfolk were considered to be socially superior to country dwellers.

Much of this changed in the second half of the 20th century with increasing competition for land. As more and more peasants started using the land of large landowners, the latter pressured the government to force the peasants to move away. This was the beginning of the slow trickle of peasants into the cities and to the forested areas in the east.

There were strict social divisions between patróns and peóns although both were of mestizo descent. Patróns were always addressed respectfully as "patrón" and rural peasants often used this form of address for anyone of higher social status. Likewise, townfolk and landowners used the term "peón" to refer to all poor people, though they would never call them this to their faces because it was offensive.

FAMILY LIFE

Family ties, even if distant, have traditionally been far more important than any other type of association in Paraguay. People depend on family connections for almost anything they need, from help finding work to money and favors. This is one fact of life that does not distinguish rich from poor or urban from rural: everyone places a great deal of importance and respect on family relationships. The rich use family connections to further their own interests, while the poor look to family to help in bad times.

The Guaraní heritage is apparent because there is slightly more emphasis on maternal relatives. From the earliest mixed marriages, the mothers obviously had more kin connections since the fathers were from Spain and arrived alone. This tradition of looking to the mother's relatives continues to the present.

The birthday girl preparing to cut the cake at her coming-of-age party.

The typical household is the nuclear family—mother, father, and their unmarried children, who usually stay home until they marry and sometimes return in the event of a divorce. The man is the acknowledged head of the household, and the woman takes care of the children and manages the finances. She maintains close ties with her own kin. If she works, she is still the primary caretaker of the children and domestic duties. The man socializes mostly outside the home. This is the traditional pattern.

About 20% of all households are headed by women: the woman lives alone with her children. After a divorce, children remain with their mother, while their father remarries or lives with his parents. There is little legal pressure for him to pay support. This is why households headed by women are among the poorest. There are few single-adult households, partly because few people can afford this and most prefer to live with relatives.

All Paraguayans are closely tied to their families.

There are three types of marriage in Paraguay: civil, religious, and consensual. The first involves acquiring a license from the state and having a ceremony with a small celebration. The second, a traditional church wedding, is usually accompanied by an expensive, elaborate reception. Consensual marriage is where the couple simply agrees to be married.

There is little difference in the status of the children of these various marriages, as long as the parents stay together and the father gives the child his last name. The only time a consensual union works to the child's disadvantage is if the father's family refuses to allow the child to use the family name or share in family inheritance at the death of the father. In this case, the child is treated almost as if it were illegitimate.

The ideal is that everyone maintains close family ties over many degrees of separation of kinship. The reality for the poor is that they have had to move around the country to find work and are often separated by long distances from their families. As a result, many of them lose touch and can trace their relations back only one generation. The rich tend to have more stable marriages and more stable lives and so maintain ties over much longer periods of time and greater degrees of separation.

In addition to ties of blood and marriage, "fictive" kinship exists in Paraguay. This is a relationship between people who are not related but behave as if they are. Fictive kinship is usually found in societies that rely heavily on kinship as a means of forming associations with one another.

FICTIVE KINSHIP

Since their ideal is to have many relatives to turn to in case of need, Paraguayans have invented ways to expand their family circle by including nonrelations or by changing distant relatives into closer ones through fictive ties. There are two ways to do this: godparenthood and adoption.

At the time a child is baptized, the parents nominate two other people, usually a married couple, to be the child's godparents. In Paraguay, the godparents have quite a lot to do with the child as he or she grows up. Parents choose godparents very carefully, and usually they seek people who are better off than themselves in the hope that the godparents will be able to help with expenses like education or healthcare throughout the child's life. In return, the child is expected to show loyalty to the godparents and help them should they request it. It was not uncommon 40 or 50 years ago for a peón to ask his patrón to be godfather to his children. This cemented patrón-peón ties and gave the children a small advantage throughout their lives.

People can also invent or change their kin relationships through adoption. The usual pattern is for wealthier urban families, related or not, to adopt a poor child from the countryside. This could be fairly informal, or be made legal. Adopted children were either those born to unwed poor mothers or into families already too big to support them. This is viewed as one way relatives, no matter how distant, can help each other out.

MEN AND WOMEN

Men are considered to be the supreme authority in their homes and in public. Men earn more than women when they work because higher-paying jobs are reserved for men and women's work is generally undervalued. About 20% of the workforce is female, and most women work in low-skilled jobs or at home doing laundry or making crafts for sale.

The role of the urban housewife is to raise children and tend the home. It is hard work, but rural women are the true backbone of the country. Not only are they expected to maintain the home, but they also do much of the field labor: haul water, collect firewood, plant crops, weed crops, harvest crops, and gather wild fruit. Men do the heavy labor: clear the land, plow it, and plant manioc. When and if women speak up about their rights, they are considered egotistical and told they are not behaving in a feminine manner. This division of labor between the sexes and all the inequalities it embodies goes back to the first European-Indian marriages where the men often treated women as only subhuman.

A mother brings her child to see the ruins near Encarnación.

In the 20th century, there were greater efforts to promote the rights of women, but the battle was slow and uphill. Paraguay was among the last countries in the Western world to give women the vote—women got the right to vote in 1963. Despite being able to vote, women hold almost no positions of public power. This is very much still a male-dominated society in all respects. Some experts argue that Paraguay's long history of brutal wars with its neighbors has made the cult of the rough, tough soldier the ideal, and that this has hindered progress in the area of women's rights.

WOMEN'S RIGHTS

It is odd that women's rights have low currency in Paraguay because women have played a greater role in its history than in many other countries in Latin America. Right from the beginning, it was the Guaraní women's kinship connections and knowledge of the environment that made the Spaniards' lives possible. As their children grew up, it was their mother's language, not their father's, that formed the basis for their ideas and culture. After the War of the Triple Alliance, it was women who rebuilt the country and kept it going, since most of the men had been killed. In the 20th century, it is still women who do most of the farm work and raise the children. Only in the public sphere do they continue to be treated as second-class citizens.

Despite this, some women stand out as committed to change. The first woman to graduate as a lawyer (in 1907) was Serafina Dávalos. Her thesis entitled "Humanism" was rediscovered by modern feminists in the 1980s. It outlines women's position in different social and economic levels and proposes radical changes to address the inequalities she witnessed.

Before the Stroessner dictatorship ended, women made only small advances, largely because they had no public power beyond the vote. This may be changing. Rodríguez' cabinet included the first female minister, Dr. Cinthia Prieto Conti, the minister of health. With a more open society and a longer experience with democracy, women may have the chance they have been waiting for to make some changes for the better.

RITES OF PASSAGE

Important milestones in a Paraguayan's life are baptism, marriage, and death. All three occasions are times when the family gathers to reassert its connections and help its members with their changing status.

Baptism is considered essential, since this is when the child is first brought to God's attention and blessed in church. Other rites prescribed by the Catholic Church include the first Holy Communion and confirmation, when children become more fully integrated into the church. Many poor people forego such rites, having little access to church or money to pay for celebrations. Marriage, as we have seen, can be more or less formal depending on financial circumstances. Funerals are similar to those in North America, except that instead of displaying the dead person in a funeral home, rural families do everything at home. Traditionally, the dead person lies in state for nine days. On the ninth night, everyone gathers to tell stories and console each other before the burial. Everyone close to the deceased is expected to wear black.

A wedding party follows the church wedding. The expense of an elaborate reception prohibits many couples from choosing to marry in church.

A teacher assists a pupil in a rural school. In Paraguay it is compulsory to attend elementary school, which lasts six years. But very few children in rural areas manage to complete even these six years.

EDUCATION

The history of education in Paraguay is one of unequal access and very slow expansion to meet the needs of the people. During the colonial period, only the very rich sent their children to school. From independence until the War of the Triple Alliance ended, educational facilities showed little progress. The single secondary school in existence closed in 1822. The only dictator of the period to do anything about education was Antonio López, who opened 400 elementary schools. By 1870, 14% of the population was literate. After the war, more effort went into improving education. The first public secondary school was opened in 1877, and the National University in Asunción was founded in 1889. In 1896 the first teacher training college opened its doors. There continued to be slow progress up to World War II, with more secondary schools and technical training schools opening. The real boost to education followed World War II—elementary school registration increased steadily then, but there was still a high degree of illiteracy in the countryside.

Currently, about 98% of children who should be in school (those between the ages of 7 and 13) register. As late as 1980, 62% of children dropped out of elementary school. Only one out of four children starting first grade eventually enrolled in secondary school. The reasons for this are numerous. There seem to be enough schools in the rural areas now, but they are seriously understaffed. If one teacher is expected to teach many students or teach multiple grades, students get little attention and learn more slowly. Rural poverty plays a big role in school dropout rates and failures. Poor families often move around in response to demand for labor. Children with no fixed address do not get registered for school. Poorer healthcare in the countryside means greater absenteeism due to illness. Finally, language is an issue: rural children speak Guaraní at home, but classroom instruction is in Spanish. Many children have a difficult time adjusting to a second language. Beyond the elementary level, the problem is worse. Only 28% of rural children of secondary school age attend school. Here the problem is one of access. There are not enough schools located within reach of rural people.

There are two universities: the National University, which is public and free, and the Catholic University, which is private. Undergraduates tend to be from the cities and come from relatively well-off families.

It has been reported that 90% of the population is literate in Spanish. This is questionable given the high dropout rates in schools. Another indication of widespread Spanish illiteracy is that Spanish-language newspapers have a circulation of only 250,000 in a population of 5.6 million. More accurate numbers suggest that about 20% of people over 10 years old are illiterate. Rural numbers are worse, about 29% of males and nearly 40% of females over 20 being illiterate. One ray of hope is that as more people move into urban areas, their access to schools will improve.

The lack of schools in Paraguay is directly related to the fact that the state does not allocate enough of its annual budget to education. Even the poorest country on the continent, Bolivia, spends twice as much proportionally on education as Paraguay does.

HEALTH

The problems affecting education can be echoed here: poverty, poor access to services in rural areas, and inadequate government spending on facilities and salaries. To begin with, there are not enough trained personnel to staff clinics and hospitals around the country. There is roughly one doctor for every 4,000 people and one nurse for every 2,000. Most of these professionals work in and around Asunción and other major urban centers. Healthcare is mostly free (there are a few private clinics for those with money), but the problem is that few of the poorest and neediest have access to it. One measure of the discrepancy in access to healthcare is the infant (0–4 years) mortality rate. The national average is 49 infant deaths per 1,000 births, but in Asunción it is only 37. This reflects greater access to healthcare and better living conditions. The primary causes of

Makeshift shantytown homes amid open drains used as sewers—such living conditions encourage the spread of disease.

SHAMANS: TRADITIONAL DOCTORS

If the rural poor are neglected by the state when it comes to healthcare, the Indians have been ignored entirely. Living as far from settlement as possible in order to protect themselves has meant that many have absolutely no state-provided healthcare. For these people, the way to treat disease is to go to the local shaman or healer. This is a person believed to be endowed with special powers. People believe that a person falls ill when a foreign object invades the body. The shaman goes into a trance in order to visualize the object and its location and then uses special chants and medicines to remove it.

Traditionally, shamans were very powerful in indigenous societies. In addition to their gift of healing the sick, they were also believed to be able to divine the future and guide the decisions of the group. People do not choose to be shamans. They are "chosen" by the spirits by being given special "sight" into the supernatural world. By going into trances, they communicate with unseen forces and use these to help them diagnose disease or predict the future.

Western medicine has long ridiculed these types of medical practitioners, and it is true that they cannot solve problems like malnutrition with their magic. However, recent studies have shown that some kinds of illnesses do respond to this type of treatment as long as the sick person really believes he or she is being cured. Some people believe that the human mind can heal the body if it is convinced that it is being healed. We may be able to learn something from these people about the power of positive thinking in the treatment of long-term diseases that do not respond to drugs or that depend on the patient's will to live.

infant and childhood deaths are diarrhea, pneumonia, malnutrition, and infections. All these are prevalent where living conditions are poor, and all can be easily treated by modern medicine. As we learned above, living conditions vary with one's proximity to a city, so once again, the rural poor suffer most.

Government spending on healthcare is inadequate to meet needs, yet it compares well with other countries in Latin America in terms of percentage of annual production. Paraguay and Chile spend the same proportion of money on healthcare, but in Chile, there is so much more money around that the sum is much higher. Paraguay, with its overall poor economy, does not produce enough to spend on services. The country has used foreign aid in recent years to try to improve the healthcare system, but it is backward in basics like vaccinations for preventable diseases such as polio and care for mothers and babies. As more people move closer to urban areas, health statistics may improve, but the 49% living in rural areas will still be left out.

Single-room homes typical of shantytowns.

HOUSING

In Paraguay, the privileged elite live in mansions that would amaze many people for their size and luxury. At the other end of the spectrum, the poor live in huts they build themselves out of whatever is available. This is true in the cities and countryside alike. Eighty percent of houses are self-built and the usual style is a one-room building made of adobe (mud bricks) with a straw or tin roof. This is one area where rural people have a slight advantage, for with lower concentrations of people living together in poor conditions, there is less risk of disease passed via rodents and insects. (This is small comfort for people living in areas with no sewers, running water, electricity, or paved roads.) Around Asunción, flooding of the major rivers in 1982 and 1983 destroyed many working class and poor neighborhoods. These still have to be rebuilt; meanwhile, people live as best as they can in temporary shacks that lack running water and sewers.

Housing is directly related to the country's health problems since many killer diseases in Paraguay can be prevented by the provision of clean water and sanitation. Diarrhea, the world's baby and child-killer, is caused by the use of contaminated water and food. Small children's bodies react to the bacteria by trying to eliminate them through the bowels. This causes dehydration, since much of the body's fluids are passed out. When more water is given, if that is contaminated too, the problem worsens and eventually the child dies of dehydration and loss of essential salts. Simply by providing clean water, many infant deaths can be prevented. Paraguay must remedy its housing situation in order to improve the country's health.

THE FIGHT FOR LAND

We have learned that many peasants in Paraguay have lost their land to large agricultural businesses as a result of Stroessner's habit of giving away large tracts of land to his friends and to foreign businesses. The plight of the peasants is sad. Another group was also affected by this land grab—the indigenous peoples in both eastern and western Paraguay. They have not only lost land, but have also been hunted, enslaved, impoverished, and robbed of their cultural roots. Here are two stories to think about.

The Achés were a group of nomadic hunter-gatherers that lived in the eastern forest region. Their language is a close relative of Guaraní and is part of the language family called Tupí-Guaraní. Unlike the Guaraní, Achés did not farm, but roamed through the forests gathering wild foods and hunting. As pressure on land use intensified in the late 1960s, this area was opened for settlers from the central zone. When they arrived, they treated the Aché like animals to be hunted down and either killed or enslaved on their farms. There is proof that 343 Indians were killed or shipped off to Asunción to be sold as virtual slaves between 1968 and 1972. Another 500 Achés have disappeared without a trace, while the few remaining Indians have been rounded up and settled on a government reserve in appalling conditions of poverty.

The Toba-Mascoy people were farmers who lived in the forbidding Chaco region. In the 1880s, when the government had to sell land to pay off the country's foreign debt, a huge section of Toba-Mascoy land was sold to an Argentinean company. With less and less land to farm, these Indians became poorer and poorer. In 1980, Stroessner agreed to give them back 25,000 acres (10,125 hectares) of land that was once theirs. One day after the 350-member community arrived to start rebuilding their lives on this land, government trucks came and took them off it again, saying that the ownership of the land was still in dispute. They were removed to a tiny camp in an area where the soil was too hard to farm. Years later, they were still waiting for resettlement; meanwhile their living conditions have gone from bad to worse.

These are only two of the unfortunate events that have occurred in Paraguay in the last 30 years. They are amazingly similar to the way indigenous people were treated in North America when it was being settled. Hundreds of years later, it appears that people still have not learned respect for indigenous peoples.

Across the country, only about 25% of households have access to clean, drinkable water. Even in Asunción, many homes do not have running water. In rural areas, only 10% of homes have running water. Another shocking statistic is that only half of all houses in the country are provided with sewage systems. The rest rely on outhouses or open sewers.

RELIGION

GUARANÍ AND SPANISH CULTURES contribute to the spiritual lives and beliefs of Paraguayans. More recently, Mennonites have made Paraguay their home and now add to this religious diversity.

NATIVE RELIGIOUS BELIEFS

Guaraní believe in the existence of gods. They call the creator of their world Ñanderuvuçú, a god living in a dark region, separated from his wife, Ñandeçy, who is known as Our Mother. Tupa, Ñandeçy's son, is the thunder god, and Yahira is the god who controls death and vengeance. Like the believers of many other religions, Guaraní pray to their gods for protection and help.

Guaraní also believe that every human has two souls: a "god-soul" that endows a person with peace, gentleness, and a craving for vegetables, and an "animal soul" that decides character. A person possessing a butterfly soul is patient and friendly, while one with a jaguar soul is cruel and brutal. Guaraní believe dreams are the souls' experiences, so they place importance on the interpretation of dreams. When a person dies, the souls are supposed to depart and go their separate ways. If the Guaraní believe the souls are hovering near the deceased, thus endangering the living, they call in shamans to perform rituals that send the souls on their way.

Finally, Guaraní believe that natural things such as plants and animals possess a spirit, which can be good or evil depending on how it is treated. As forest dwellers, Guaraní believe that the natural world must be treated with respect in order not to offend these spirits.

Above: **Catholic priests hear confession outdoors as crowds await their turn.**

Opposite: **Souvenir stands near the Basílica of Our Lady of the Miracles in Caacupé, Paraguay's most important religious center.**

A mural depicting rural Catholicism in a church in the town of San Juan Bautista.

CATHOLICISM

About 90–97% of the population are Roman Catholic. Despite this, the Catholic Church has not played as large a role in Paraguayan life and politics as it has in other Latin American countries. In the colonial period, Paraguay was the site of the first diocese created in South America (1547). Travel was so difficult that only half of the first 40 bishops assigned to Asunción arrived. The Catholic Church in Paraguay was often leaderless. After independence, Francia confiscated church lands and closed religious schools. Successive dictators were not as antireligious, but it was not until 1894 that another bishop was assigned to Paraguay. People remained Catholic, but participation in church activities declined for lack of priests. From the turn of the 20th century until Stroessner's regime, the Catholic Church stayed out of politics.

After a meeting of Latin American Catholic bishops in Medellín, Colombia, in 1968, the Catholic Church became more involved in politics, pledging itself to help the poor and stand up for the rights of the abused.

From 1968, priests worked with labor unions to help rural workers, organized Christian American Leagues to bring literacy and health services to the poor, and tried to get workers to organize themselves into unions to fight for their rights. Stroessner responded with repression, arresting or exiling many League leaders. In the 1970s church-state relations worsened. The archbishop refused to sit on the Council of State, citing human rights abuse, and even excommunicated members of Stroessner's government responsible for deaths and torture. Near the end of Stroessner's regime, the Catholic Church organized the National Dialogue—discussions among social and political leaders to criticize Stroessner, which he strongly resented. Things came to a head with the visit of Pope John Paul II in 1988. Throughout his stay, the Pope talked about the need for a better human rights record and more freedom of speech and political participation. He gave his support to Catholic groups representing the poor and repressed. When Rodríguez took over in 1989, he promised to improve church-state relations. The Catholic Church's strong reputation among citizens for its work on their behalf gives it political weight.

The role of the church in everyday life is to provide a focus for community activities. People celebrate important saints' days as a group and place importance on religious rites of passage, such as baptism, when people gather to celebrate the change in status of one of their members. Generally, women are more involved in church activities than men and attend Mass more regularly.

Pope John Paul II receives a birthday gift from two children in Encarnación. Stroessner tried to stop a planned meeting between the Pope and the political opposition. When the Pope responded by threatening to cancel his visit altogether, Stroessner backed down.

79

During their brief existence, Reductions demonstrated that Indians and Europeans could live in a single community based on mutual respect and prosper.

THE REDUCTIONS Although the Catholic Church was generally not involved in the lives of Paraguayans until modern times, this was not true for Indians during the colonial period. A group of priests called Jesuits (from Society of Jesus) started working with Indians in Brazil in 1607. They soon realized that European settlers were regularly rounding up thousands of Guaraní for slave labor on their farms. The Jesuits decided to remove the Indians from contact with Europeans. In 1609 they began to build Guaraní communities known as Reductions; eventually there were more than 30 in eastern Paraguay, northwest Argentina, and southwest Brazil. These missions were to educate Indians in Catholicism, teach them basic skills and trades, and protect them from Europeans.

More than 1,500 Jesuits from all over Europe dedicated their lives to Reductions. The work was hard and many died of disease or exhaustion. Each Reduction held 2,000–4,000 Indians and was self-sufficient in food and clothing. They also devoted part of each day to education and to learning Guaraní ways. The Jesuits were the first to try to record a Guaraní dictionary.

REDUCTIONS PAST AND PRESENT

Though the Jesuit missions called Reductions were left in ruins for a long time, archeologists have started working in them to learn how the Indians lived.

From the remains, we know that the church was the biggest and most central Reduction building. It dominated the central plaza or square. On either side of the church was the cemetery and the priests' residence. Also on the main square was the school, workshops, and the "big house" for orphans and widows. Guaraní families each had a small house or segment of a long, subdivided house for their own use. There were common areas around these dwellings so that people could live and work together as they had been accustomed to doing in the forest. Behind the church was the garden. Land in the Reduction was commonly owned and worked. Every family contributed labor to mission activities and no one owned the products of their own labor. This communal system is part of the reason that the missions were so successful. The Guaraní did not have a strong sense of private property and worked well as a group. The missions were so productive that they often sold extra food and manufactured items to other Europeans. The Jesuits forbade any other Europeans to live in the Reductions, thereby protecting the Indians from negative influence. Many Guaraní became amazing craftsmen and women under the tutelage of the Jesuits.

Life was strict but fair and the native people were not forced to stay in the missions—they simply preferred it to living in constant fear for their lives. Today, a few of the bigger missions have been partially restored so that visitors can see for themselves what life was like.

Many have argued that the Jesuits were too paternalistic, assuming the role of parents over their Indian "children." This is correct to some extent, but the Reductions were the only thing that saved the lives of some 80,000 Indians who otherwise would have been enslaved or killed. As the Reductions flourished in the 1700s, European settlers became envious of their success and of the power of the Jesuits in Latin America. Back in Europe, people started agitating with the Spanish king to get rid of them. The Europeans wanted not only the land in the Reductions, but also the labor of the Indians there.

By 1767, they were successful; the Jesuits were forced to leave the Reductions and South America. Without the priests to lead and protect them, the Indians dispersed, and many were forced to work on European farms. Some wandered back into the forest, but many ended up in Asunción looking for work. This was a sad moment for the Guaraní. The Reduction buildings fell into disrepair and were looted by settlers to build their own houses. Francia went so far as to destroy many Reduction buildings, and Antonio López confiscated all remaining Reduction lands.

"Our purpose in establishing the Reductions is to achieve peace between the Indians and the Spaniards. This is a difficult task."

"We work for justice. ... Indians need to be freed from the slavery and harsh personal servitude in which they now exist."

—Comments from two early Jesuit priests

SYNCRETISM: MESTIZO RELIGION

When two cultures coexist for a long time, elements of each are often combined to form a new blend. This process, called syncretism, is part of Paraguayan culture today. The mestizo majority show many cultural elements from both their Guaraní heritage and their Spanish history. One area where this is obvious is in religion. Mestizos are Roman Catholics now, but some of their beliefs reflect Guaraní religious beliefs. For example, many rural people fear the evil spirits of Guaraní folklore. Here is the story of how some of these evil spirits were created.

A long time ago, an extraordinarily beautiful girl was born. The evil god Tau decided he wanted her and attacked her. Arasy, a female god, cursed him so that the girl's union with Tau produced seven evil and monstrous sons. One was a huge lizard with seven dog heads. The second was a serpent with a parrot's beak. The third was also a serpent but with horns and dangerous teeth. The fourth was a little man with golden hair who could make himself invisible. The fifth was a god who ate humans. The sixth attacked women and children. The seventh, Luisón, a wolf-man, was the god of the night and accompanied death. He liked to wander around cemeteries.

Rural mestizos still fear these gods and demons and sometimes claim to hear them, especially Luisón, as they pass near bushes at night.

OTHER RELIGIONS

Besides the very few indigenous peoples that have held on to their beliefs, the only other religion represented in Paraguay is Protestant Christianity. This is represented by two groups: the Mennonites, who practice a very old form of Protestantism, and modern Protestant missionaries of North American evangelical churches, who work among rural and indigenous peoples.

The evangelical churches have been trying to convert the rural poor and especially poor Indians to their faith. Some criticize their involvement with indigenous groups, claiming that they have helped the government subdue and repress indigenous culture. Other than Mennonites, Protestants are still a very small minority in Paraguay.

MENNONITES are a Protestant sect founded in Europe in 1526. They believe in strict adherence to the scriptures and adult baptism, and are pacifists. Over the centuries, Mennonites have migrated to places that will let them live as they choose. At the turn of the 20th century, Mennonites in Canada, Germany, and Russia were forced to move. Two destinations in Latin America at the time were very popular: Mexico and Paraguay.

Paraguay was attractive because it had lots of unused land in the Chaco and the government promised to let them live as they wanted. They did not have to do military service or pay taxes, but were responsible for their own German-language schools and local law enforcement. The first group came from Canada in 1927 and founded a settlement at Loma Plata. The second group, from Russia, founded Filadelfia in the 1930s. Finally, in 1947, a third group arrived who had been forced to serve in the German army during World War II. They settled at Neu-Halbstadt.

Although the government gave them guarantees that they could live as they chose, the Mennonites soon realized they had been settled in an area that was by no means peaceful. The Chaco was disputed by Bolivians and Paraguayans during the Chaco War and Chaco Indian groups were not always happy to see the new settlers. Over time, a relationship developed between Mennonites and Indians: those Indians who wanted to convert to the Mennonite religion were welcome to settle alongside the Mennonites, though they had to maintain their own church. Non-Christian Indians—those who had not settled—worked as part-time laborers for the Mennonites.

An auction at a Mennonite festival in Filadelfia. The Mennonite communities are quite prosperous, having worked very hard to become successful farmers in the unforgiving Chaco. Many younger Mennonites have learned passable Spanish, and in this way there has been some cultural integration.

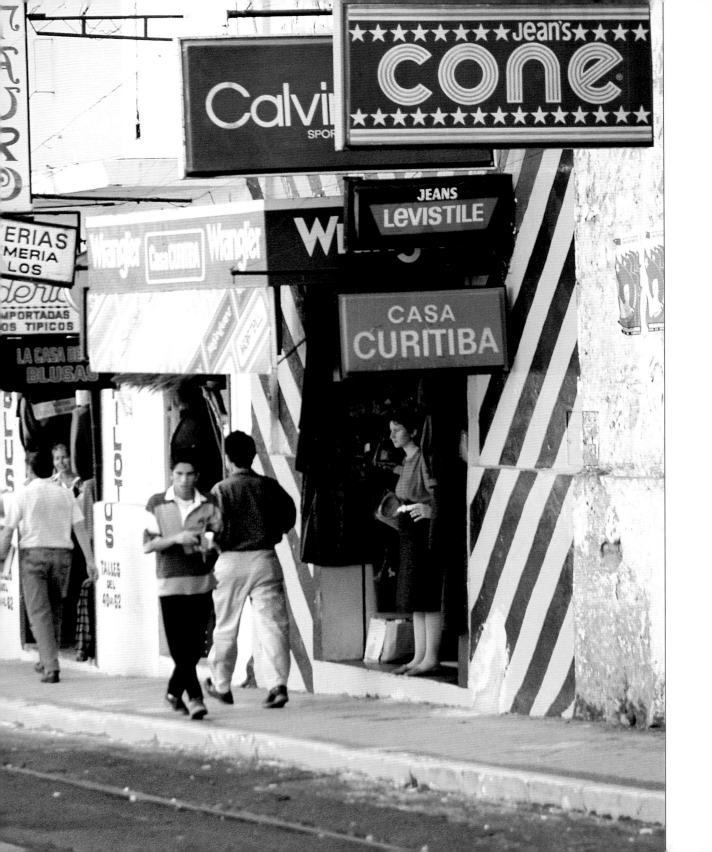

LANGUAGE

UNLIKE ALL OF ITS NEIGHBORS, Paraguay has a native Indian language as one of two official languages. This chapter will focus on how this works and the way Paraguayans perceive their two languages.

NATIONAL LANGUAGES

Two official languages are recognized in Paraguay's 1967 constitution: Spanish and Guaraní. Spanish is the language of government and education, and the dominant language of commerce. Guaraní is the language of everyday life for most people. Paraguay is the only country in the Western Hemisphere whose daily language is an aboriginal one rather than a European import. At least 90% of Paraguayans can speak Guaraní at some level. Only 6% are monolingual Spanish speakers and about 50% are bilingual in both national languages. In Asunción, 71% of residents speak both languages, while in some rural areas only Guaraní is spoken. An interesting statistic is that 70% of 3 and 4-year-old children speak only Guaraní. This suggests that Guaraní is the predominant home language. All of Paraguay's presidents have been able to speak Guaraní, and many have used this to gain popularity.

Official policy on the value of Guaraní has changed over the years. After independence, the use of Guaraní in the classroom was banned. This did nothing to change the national language because so few people went to school then. When Antonio López expanded education in rural areas, Spanish was the only language of instruction. His son, Solano López, used Guaraní as a symbol of nationalism—something that made Paraguayans distinct from Argentineans and Uruguayans (two of Paraguay's three enemies in the War of the Triple Alliance).

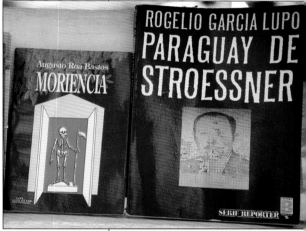

Above and opposite: **Most Paraguayan books and shop signs are in Spanish.**

Posters and prints for sale in Asunción.

When Paraguay lost the war, Guaraní was once again scorned by the new elite, who tried to copy the Argentineans in matters of culture. While Guaraní had no social status in the late 19th and early 20th centuries, most rural people continued to speak it and were largely monolingual. Spanish was heard only among the wealthy of Asunción. During the Chaco War, Paraguayan generals realized that they could use Guaraní to prevent the Bolivians from understanding their orders. They forbade the use of Spanish on the battlefield, and when Paraguay won the war, the use of Guaraní became a matter of national pride.

This flip-flopping of attitudes is reflected in modern Paraguayans' perception of Guaraní. Spanish is the language of educated people, and the Guaraní word for "Spanish language" means "language of the masters." Knowledge of Spanish gives a person extra social status, and to participate in business or politics, one must speak it well. At the same time, Guaraní is known as the language of the people, and it would be difficult to live without it in the rural areas. Even in urban centers, most Paraguayans think in Guaraní and translate their thoughts into Spanish.

National Languages

As they usually learn Guaraní first in the context of family life, Paraguayans' most emotional thoughts and ideas are more easily expressed in Guaraní than in Spanish, which they learn in the formal setting of a classroom. For this reason, Guaraní poetry is very popular. One of Paraguay's most accomplished writers in Spanish, Augusto Roa Bastos, admits thinking in Guaraní and then translating thoughts into Spanish. Some experts argue that most Paraguayans are not truly bilingual but are Guaraní speakers who learned Spanish as a second language and are never able to think in Spanish. That may be, but there is no thriving Guaraní literature, and all daily newspapers are in Spanish. It seems Paraguayans are not quite ready to admit being first and foremost Guaraní speakers. This may be because they feel at some level that Guaraní is an Indian language and therefore not as prestigious as Spanish.

One issue that continues to be debated in Paraguay is whether or not to standardize Guaraní spelling and grammar. Guaraní has absorbed many Spanish words and forms of pronunciation over the years. Traditionalists think this is the way it should be spelled and written; they do not want to change the idiosyncrasies of the language, as they feel this gives the language its character. Others feel there should be a standard Guaraní that is written according to scientific rules. This would eliminate confusing and contradictory spellings and grammatical forms that have resulted from the blending of Spanish and Guaraní.

English also has its traditionalists. Americans spell words as they sound and have dropped some of the extra letters found in British English. British and Canadian English retains older versions of spelling on the grounds that this is how the language was traditionally written: *neighbor* is spelled *neighbour*, and *theater* spelled *theatre*. The debate in Paraguay is still unresolved.

Paraguayans have contradictory feelings about their two national languages. Many feel that Spanish is the language of superior people. At the same time, Guaraní is what makes them distinctly Paraguayan. Pride in Guaraní is in conflict with their perception that it is inferior to the borrowed European language.

SPEECH PATTERNS AND LANGUAGE USAGE

There are significant differences between urban and rural Paraguayans in many areas: one of them is in the use of the two national languages. In large urban centers, about 30% of families prefer to use Spanish as their home language, 20% prefer Guaraní, and the rest use both freely at home. In rural areas, only 2% of families prefer Spanish, 75% prefer Guaraní, and 23% use both interchangeably at home. This difference reflects different levels of access to education and different levels of educational achievement.

TUPÍ-GUARANÍ

Tupí-Guaraní is the name of the linguistic family that includes Guaraní. Before the Europeans arrived, Guaraní people had expanded their territory to include a large segment of the coast of modern Brazil, and from the Atlantic Ocean all the way inland to the Paraná, Uruguay, and Paraguay rivers. Numerically, they formed the biggest indigenous group in this region. For this reason, Guaraní was the first, and sometimes the only, native language used by conquistadores and Spanish priests trying to convert the Indians to Christianity. The Jesuits created the first dictionaries of Guaraní and Guaraní is still spoken widely today.

These few words and phrases in Guaraní will give you an idea of how the language sounds:

English	Guaraní	Pronunciation
I	che	"chay"
you	nde	"nday"
we	ñande	"NYAN-day"
big	guazú	"gwah-ZOO"
small	mishí	"mee-SHEE"
hot	hakú	"hah-KOO"
cold	roí	"roh-EE"
How are you?	Mba'eichapa?	"mbah ay-ee-CHAH-pah?"
Fine, and you?	Iporaiterei, ha nde?	"ee-por-ay-ee-tayr-AY-ee, hah nday?"

Among Paraguayans who can speak Spanish (this is about half the population), there are big differences in how Spanish is spoken, depending on where the person lives and how well educated he or she is. The elite of the country speak Spanish as well as any other Spanish-speaking group in Latin America; this is a very small group though.

The majority of Paraguayans speak a type of Spanish that is influenced by Guaraní. The group with the least amount of education and fluency in Spanish will often mix the two languages, using Guaraní words and Spanish words together in one sentence with a grammatical form that suits the words they have chosen. This total mixture of languages is called *guarañol* ("gwar-ahn-YOHL"), and some experts have suggested that it is a third, separate language. In between fluent speakers of Spanish and guarañol speakers are "bilinguals"—those capable of speaking both languages well. They often switch to another language in mid-sentence, but always use the correct grammar for whatever language they are speaking. This is called code-switching and is an interesting habit among bilingual populations.

The Mennonites may converse in German in the town of Filadelfia, but the signs are in Spanish, an indication that the Mennonites have integrated culturally to some extent.

When one language is more valued (Spanish in this example) than the other, there are distinct patterns in code-switching. The valued language is used in formal circumstances, like talking to one's boss or discussing intellectual subjects, while the other language is used among friends in social situations, at home, or when joking. Sometimes people code-switch in mid-conversation. This is because they find it easier to express themselves on different topics in one or the other language. This happens especially when only one language is taught in school or published in books and newspapers (as is mostly the case in Paraguay). Thus, when people are talking about their everyday lives they tend to use Guaraní, but when they want to talk about the news or academic subjects, they switch to Spanish.

Some Guaraní words that have become a permanent part of Paraguayan Spanish include *ñandú* ("nyan-DOO," rhea), *ñandutí* (Paraguayan lace), *yopará* ("yo-pah-RAH," a jungle vine), and many other words for animals, plants, and weather patterns. A speaker of standard Spanish who listens to Paraguayans speak their version of Spanish could be quite confused. Likewise, Guaraní has picked up Spanish words and pronunciations over five centuries of contact between the two languages: it is no longer the Guaraní that was spoken when the Spaniards first arrived. Language is one of the most dynamic areas of Paraguayan culture.

OTHER LANGUAGES

Due to the isolation of much of the countryside throughout most of its history, other languages have survived in

Paraguayan Spanish adopts the Guaraní word for the rhea: *ñandú*.

Paraguay. Aside from Guaraní, at least four other native languages are still spoken in the Chaco region. These languages have survived because their speakers have been left alone for most of the last 500 years. During the 20th century, these native groups have been forced to have more contact with non-native peoples, including Guaraní and Spanish-speaking mestizos and German-speaking Mennonites. Now, many of them are bilingual in at least one other language, often Guaraní.

LANGUAGE AND STATUS

Part of the mixed feelings Paraguayans have about the Guaraní language has to do with their perception of Guaraní as "only an Indian language," while Spanish is seen as the "language of masters." This association of languages with status is quite common around the world. All languages are equally good, useful, and sophisticated, but for some reason, people continue to rank them as better or worse depending on how their speakers are ranked socially. Indians are definitely second-class citizens in Paraguay, so not surprisingly, Indian languages are also rated second-class.

In the United States, there is a similar phenomenon with regard to the type of English people speak. Generally, the English of well-educated white people is considered to be "proper" English, while the versions spoken by poorer people and African-Americans from the inner cities is thought to be "bad" English. Experts in the study of languages (linguists) do not agree. They have studied African-American English and say it has its own grammar and vocabulary. This grammar is different from standard English because it has been influenced by African languages, but it is a perfectly good grammar, and speakers of this type of English can think and say complicated things just as speakers of any language can. Unfortunately, because African-American people have often been treated as second-class citizens, it is assumed that their language is also second-class. This creates a vicious circle: when they speak, listeners think they do not speak proper English and so conclude that they must be inferior people.

Respect for all languages and their speakers is important, if only because the variety of languages in existence is one of the richest treasures in the world and worth preserving.

Stroessner did not care much about the rights or culture of Paraguay's remaining indigenous peoples and consequently they were under constant threat of cultural destruction. The democratic Paraguayan state that followed, beginning with Wasmosy, has made greater efforts to protect indigenous groups and thereby help to preserve their languages.

Besides Spanish, other non-native languages are spoken in Paraguay. The largest group, the German-speaking Mennonites, came to Paraguay in part because the government promised them that they could continue to speak their form of German. There are Mennonite schools that teach German in their settlements.

The Japanese have also retained the use of their language. At first, they taught their children only Japanese, but more recently they decided to integrate more fully with Paraguayan society. Now children of Japanese descent learn in Spanish while Japanese is taught as a second language.

ARTS

FINE ARTS IN PARAGUAY do not have a long tradition, and art at the formal level has not been much in evidence. Directly after gaining independence, Paraguay fell under the control of the dictator, Francia. He not only closed the borders to prevent any contact with larger populations in Buenos Aires and around the world, he also closed the schools. He was quite an educated and literate person, but he preferred to be the only one in the country who was and systematically jailed and killed most other educated Europeans in Paraguay at the time.

The arts did not begin to recover from this isolation until after the War of the Triple Alliance (1864–70). Even now, Paraguay has an under-developed artistic community. In the 20th century, unstable and repressive governments, especially Stroessner's, muffled literary and artistic aspirations. Finally, the predominantly rural character and poverty of the population has meant that there has been only a very small nucleus of people with

Left: **Indian handicraft at the Plaza de los Héroes, the central square of Asunción.**

Opposite: **A woman in Itauguá making *ñandutí*, Paraguay's "spider web lace."**

the education and experience to appreciate fine art and therefore promote it in the country. With a new, more open system and efforts directed at educating the population, formal or fine arts may finally get the attention they deserve.

Having said that, Paraguay has a vibrant and colorful tradition of folk or people's art, and many of its crafts rival any in the world for their beauty and distinctiveness.

LITERARY ARTS

The first real wave of Paraguayan writers is known as "The Generation of 1870" because they all started writing after the end of the Triple Alliance War. These men (there were no women) combined writing with politics and the latter usually influenced the former.

Augusto Roa Bastos was exiled in the civil unrest that followed the Chaco War. More than any other modern author, he describes Paraguayan reality and culture to the rest of the world.

One writer and art patron of this epoch was Juan Silvano Godoi. Another influential writer and politician of the era was Cecilio Báez, born in 1862 and a lawyer by profession. He wrote for newspapers and advocated democracy and free trade rules as the answer to Paraguay's continual political turmoil. He was responsible for the formal organization of the Liberal Party in 1887 and was instrumental in overthrowing the Colorados in 1904.

Like Báez, most other writers of this generation were Liberals, and many of them held important government positions or were quite powerful behind the scenes. Most of the books published in this period were histories of Paraguay or political commentaries on the future of Paraguay. They are characterized by their extreme patriotism and rather biased interpretations of history.

ROA BASTOS

Augusto Roa Bastos was born in Paraguay in 1917 and raised by his uncle, a bishop, in the jungle. Like many of his generation, he fought in the Chaco War and was permanently altered by his experiences of violence and brutality there. He started writing as a young man and continued when he returned from the war, though he never completed his education. His first novel was never published, although it won a local literary prize.

He worked as a journalist for an Asunción paper and was sent to Europe to cover World War II. When he returned to Paraguay in 1945, he was exiled for political reasons and for some time lived in Buenos Aires. There he continued writing and became involved with the Argentine motion picture industry. Some of his books have been made into films. In 1960 he published *Son of Man*, a novel about the Chaco War that was later translated into English. The book is about one individual's struggle for freedom and how solidarity among people can spring from adversity. His most acclaimed novel, *I, the Supreme*, is about Paraguay's first dictator, Francia. It was first published in 1974 and translated into English in 1986. He has taught in France, and his work has been highlighted in American literature programs. He has been able to return to Paraguay since Stroessner was overthrown but continues to live in France.

In the 20th century, a new generation of writers emerged that was largely the product of the Chaco War. This war was very significant to Paraguayans, as it was to Bolivians. Many people were forced to think long and hard about their country's history and its future. In North America and Europe, a parallel can be drawn with the Great War (World War I) since it was so traumatic for all people involved that it sparked a change in outlook. The same can be said for the participants in the Chaco War.

These new writers tended to focus on fiction rather than history, but they were also drawn into politics, mostly by virtue of being exiled from the country by one or more regimes. Stroessner was particularly intolerant, so some of Paraguay's best 20th century writers have lived most of their lives outside Paraguay. Roa Bastos is a good example. Another is Gabriel Casaccia, born in Asunción in 1907 and by 1935 exiled to Argentina. All of his novels were published in Buenos Aires and all deal with the hopelessness of the politically and morally corrupt society in Paraguay. He died in 1980, never having returned to his country.

Poetry has also had some success in the 20th century, with the works of Roa Bastos and Josefina Plá being the most notable. Literary observers are waiting to see if democracy will revive the literary tradition in Paraguay.

JOSEFINA PLÁ

Paraguay's best-known and most influential female artist and cultural expert, Josefina Plá, was born in the Canary Islands in 1909 and came to Paraguay with her husband in 1927. Her earliest artistic endeavors were in poetry. Her first volume of poems, *The Price of Dreams*, was published in 1934. During the Chaco War, she operated a radio station that presented dramas and comedies to the soldiers in the field. While organizing this, she brought together a variety of writers and actors who later formed the nucleus of Paraguay's postwar cultural scene.

Her talents do not stop at poetry and organizing: she is also a sculptor whose work has been exhibited all over South America, and her murals and mosaics decorate important buildings in Asunción. Josefina Plá is also a historian. She has written two books on the art of Paraguay: one on the art of the Jesuit missions and the other on plastic arts in Paraguay. Her most recent book, published in 1984, is about the British in Paraguay. She also writes for the newspapers on a regular basis. She is truly the grand dame of the Paraguayan art scene.

Opposite: **A 17th century Franciscan church carving by Guaraní. The best examples of Guaraní religious art are found in the Jesuit missions.**

The Guaraní were taught a Baroque style of carving popular in Europe in the 17th century. Unlike the Classical style, which is simple and ordered, the Baroque is detailed and fluid. Carvings in this style often have complicated designs of leaves and vines twisting among angels or saints.

VISUAL ARTS

Godoi established the first museum featuring visual art, which he had to bring from abroad as there was nothing Paraguayan to display at the turn of the 20th century. In the first three decades of the century, under Liberal rule, there was some interest in art exhibitions of local works. The first, held in 1918, attracted 209 paintings. Some artists of Paraguayan nationality who had been studying and exhibiting abroad returned to show their work for the first time. Two of these were Jaime Bestard and Juan Samudio.

The first woman painter to show her work in Asunción was Ofelia Echague Vera. She held her own exhibition in 1945 and met with some success. Her work is characterized as "feminine," which may be why she was successful. In 1936 Wolf Bandurek, a Jew, emigrated to Paraguay from Germany, seeking refuge from the Nazis. His artwork is very dark and full of the terror of Nazi Germany. Josefina Plá, a sculptor and mosaic-maker, has been instrumental in bringing together people interested in promoting Paraguayan art at home and abroad.

As with all things artistic, the Stroessner years were not particularly productive of visual art. There were few artists in that era, and they had to contend with an indifferent state unwilling to fund projects or displays. Today, however, the Barro Museum in Asunción exhibits art from colonial to modern times, emphasizing modern and unconventional works of art.

GUARANÍ-BAROQUE The two most famous Jesuit Reductions in Paraguay are Jesús and Trinidad. Both are preserved as historic sites and are reminders of the miracles worked by the Jesuits and Guaraní people in the forests of eastern Paraguay. The main church and school buildings were all made of stone that was hand-cut and carried to the site. Their architecture shows how creative the designers could be using simple tools and materials. In addition, church pulpits and arches are exquisitely carved with angels and other religious icons. In 1981 a collection of wooden statues was discovered in a burial tunnel in Trinidad. This is a veritable treasure, since most portable objects had long since been stolen and sold. The style of wood and stone carving is so distinct that art historians have given it its own name: Guaraní-Baroque.

Guaraní carving is distinctive, reflecting both the Baroque style taught to them by the priests and their own vision of the natural world. The life-size statues of saints are said to capture emotions in their faces and are considered to be some of the finest religious art in the world. The fact that such beautiful artwork came from these places and times suggests that the missions were real havens for the Guaraní who were allowed to express themselves in a safe and loving environment.

Above: **A band plays Paraguayan music using a harp and guitars.**

Opposite: **The** *galopa* **("gah-LOH-pah") is a graceful dance for women only and involves some complicated balancing.**

PERFORMING ARTS

THEATER Asunción is Paraguay's center for the performing arts. There is a lively theater scene with productions in both Spanish and Guaraní. The first play in Guaraní, written by Julie Correa, was put on during the Chaco War in 1933. It was about the war and attracted crowds so large that the police had to be called in to manage them. This success derives in part from people's nationalism during wartime and in part from the use of the Guaraní language. People spoke better Guaraní than Spanish then, and clearly they supported theater in their home language.

MUSIC Two types of music are typically Paraguayan: the polka and the *guarania* ("gwar-ah-NEE-ah"). Polkas are adaptations of eastern European musical forms and dances. Guaranias are the love songs traditionally sung by a suitor to his beloved outside her window at night. This music uses a particularly Paraguayan ensemble of guitars and the Paraguayan harp, which looks much like the European harp of large symphonies, but is made differently and sounds different. Many restaurants feature guitar and harp ensembles to entertain their guests. The Ballet Folklorico (Folkloric Ballet) holds frequent music and dance performances to preserve the tradition of the performing arts.

LA GALOPA is a special dance performed by women only. It has gone out of fashion as a regular feature of rural life, but the Folkloric Ballet still performs it for tourists and Paraguayans. The dancers dress in typical 19th century rural costume and step to polka-like music while balancing bottles on their heads. A *galopera* (galopa dancer) may have as many as 10 bottles balanced while dancing. The bottles are all attached to each other but not to her head, which makes balancing pretty tricky.

The galopa originated as a dance for particular saints' days. Women would pray to saints for specific things; if they got them, they would dance at the festival to thank the saint. To make this more difficult, they would dance with a jug filled with water on their heads. When they finished the dance, they would offer the water to spectators, saying "thank you, Saint Blaise" or "thank you, Holy Virgin" as each person drank from the jug. When they finished, they felt they had "paid" the saint back for whatever they had received. Sometimes, women would dance just to show their faith to the saint.

FOLK ART

There is a wealth of handicrafts and folk art produced in Paraguay that can be divided by medium, starting with textiles.

TEXTILES The most famous of Paraguay's handmade textiles is ñandutí, the "spider's web" cotton lace for which the town of Itauguá is famous. *Ahó poí* ("ah-HOH POY") is a very fine handwoven cotton fabric first made when Francia closed the country's borders. Once denied access to imports, people had to manufacture their own cloth. The national dress is usually made with ahó poí. A rougher form of handmade cotton cloth is the *poyvi* ("poy-VEE"). It is the material for ponchos, hammocks, and rugs rather than fine clothing. Sheep were introduced to the country in the 17th century and since then there have been woolens produced by hand and now by machine.

LEATHER With the introduction of cattle, leather working developed. The Jesuit missions were famous for their finely crafted leather, but such skills were lost with the death of craftsmen during the Triple Alliance War. Leather working was revived in the 20th century, and Paraguayan products such as shoes and bags rival those from Argentina and Brazil.

THE SPIDER'S WEB

Paraguay's most famous folk art is ñandutí, which is the Guaraní word for "spider's web." It is a lace made from cotton. Women make it using a wooden frame and remove the frame when it is completed. Ñandutí production is one of the home industries that supplement family earnings. It is highly prized by Paraguayans and tourists alike.

There are many theories about its origin. The first record of ñandutí is in 1728 in the town of Itauguá. Some experts say it is an adaptation of a lace made in the Canary Islands and brought over during migrations of Canary Islanders. Others think it may be an adaptation of a textile made by Guaraní out of cotton thread. Whatever its origins, the themes are definitely influenced by mestizo culture since they often include images of nature such as flowers and birds.

Ñandutí was first made primarily to adorn churches and altars. Since the beginning of the 20th century, it has become popular as trimming on clothing and as home decoration.

WOODWORK The most famous woodwork comes from the Chaco Indians, who carve an aromatic wood called *palo santo* ("PAH-loh SAHN-toh") into animal shapes and replicas of hunting weapons. In Luque, craftsmen make beautiful guitars and harps. Finally, the Guaraní statues made in Reductions are being revived as a folk art in Tobatí, where people use the same techniques and colors to create replicas of religious icons.

POTTERY is a thriving folk art and home industry. Women are the potters, and their art reflects the Guaraní heritage. Most of today's ceramic ware is produced as art rather than for utility. The typical theme is the female figure in a variety of poses. Not so long ago, most houses had to collect water or have it delivered, and the water was stored in large jars. Modern potters are still making fanciful and beautiful jars as collector's pieces.

BASKETRY is still a viable cottage industry for women. Guaraní crafts-women taught their children how to work with the fibers of plants such as the coconut palm and jungle vines.

JEWELRY Last but not least is metalwork. Paraguay's jewelers are famous for gold and silver filigree work. Designs are made from wire twisted into complicated swirls and patterns and then formed into shapes either for use as jewelry or in home decoration. Filigree can also be wrapped around another material like wood, horn, or glass to decorate containers such as glasses and sugar bowls.

Opposite: **Hammocks made of** *poyví* **cloth are sold in Itauguá.**

LEISURE

FOR THE POOREST IN PARAGUAY, leisure is not an option: survival requires work and more work. Historically, this was also true for peasants in Europe. Only recently in Western history have people become accustomed to regular breaks from work. We think of these intervals as leisure time and generally take it for granted. In affluent countries, whole industries are devoted to creating activities for people at leisure—sports clubs, television networks, movie industries, and computer game designers, for example.

Above: **Village bingo, a time to gather for a little fun.**

Opposite: **Teen leisure for the elite in urban centers of Paraguay is much the same as in other cities.**

To understand the concept of leisure in a country as poor and rural as Paraguay, one must start by recognizing that all these leisure activities are modern luxuries enjoyed by only a few people around the world. This is not to suggest that life is never fun for Paraguayans, only that the way many entertain themselves is not as much a part of daily life as leisure has become for some of us.

SPORTS

Poverty and location often affect the choice of activity. For example, Paraguayans enjoy swimming as a pastime, but this pleasure is more accessible to rural people living near rivers than to the urban poor.

The most popular sport in Paraguay, as in much of the less developed world, is soccer. This game became popular with schoolboys in England in the mid-1800s. Its simplicity and affordability soon made it popular with the working class. The game began to spread around the world in the late 1800s. It became popular in Latin America near the turn of the 20th century and is now the sport of choice for the vast majority of boys in South America. Soccer's widespread appeal is due to the fact that no special

Enthusiasm for soccer is widespread, and im- promptu games occur everywhere, since only formal matches require 11 players to a side.

equipment is needed. Any ball of approximately the right size and weight will work, and it can be made out of locally available materials. Any piece of relatively flat land is the only other thing required, plus enthusiastic players, of course! Often, whether or not a boy plays soccer depends on whether he lives near enough to a town or school with a field.

Paraguay has amateur teams as well as professional teams that compete in international soccer matches. There is a stadium in Asunción and residents enjoy attending games or watching them on television. Since many people cannot afford their own television, men especially often watch the game at a local bar. Television is nearly nonexistent among peasants so their substitute is the radio. Again, men often gather in a public spot to listen to the game and socialize.

Sports preferred by the wealthy include golf, basketball, and horseracing. Basketball was only recently introduced to South America via satellite television, but it is gaining popularity. Golf is one of the world's more expensive sports. Equipment is complicated and pricey as are golf club memberships. This sport is not for the average Paraguayan.

LEISURE ACTIVITIES

Among rich Paraguayans, going to the movies and watching television are popular. Paraguay is too small to support its own movie industry, so movies are imported from Argentina and the United States. English films are screened with Spanish subtitles. Only large population centers have theaters. For the majority there is the radio, but even this exceeds many budgets. Some of Paraguay's rural areas are very remote. Electricity is not necessarily available and batteries are costly. In such places leisure usually means passing the time of day with neighbors.

The wealthy enjoy tourism in their own country. They make trips to the national parks or to less settled areas to fish or hunt. Fishing is particularly good in Paraguay and attracts fishing enthusiasts from abroad.

TOURISM IN PARAGUAY

Most Paraguayans cannot afford to explore their own country, but some foreigners find their way to the heart of South America. In fact, tourism provides about 22% of Paraguay's annual income. The number of foreign tourist arrivals each year is small, about 330,000, but it generates about US$150 million in income each year. Now that Paraguay is no longer under the shadow of military control, more people will want to visit.

Most visitors come from neighboring countries. For some, the attraction is cheaper shopping. Paraguay also has well-preserved national parks that attract wealthy tourists interested in ecotourism, a recent phenomenon that has become popular around the world wherever there are natural environments. This type of tourism aims to let people enjoy nature without disturbing it.

Besides natural wonders, Paraguay also offers visitors a taste of a different culture. For other Latin Americans, Paraguay is considered exotic because of its blend of Guaraní and Spanish cultures. One of the national cultural treasures is the collection of Jesuit Reductions found in the eastern region; the government has declared them protected sites and is trying to raise money to restore them properly to attract tourists. North Americans are also attracted by Paraguayan culture, though few can afford the time and money to make their way to this strange and amazing place.

Throughout the year everyone celebrates various festivals, the extent of their participation being guided by their means. In between, family rituals provide diversion. A baptism or marriage, for example, is a social event for neighbors to help out and enjoy the festivities.

Some Guaraní games have survived in the countryside. One game is similar to badminton, except that no racket or net is used. The shuttlecock is made from corn leaves and the object of the game is to hit it back and forth using the hands, without letting it fall to the ground.

STORYTELLING

For those who cannot afford organized leisure activities, there is always the age-old entertainment provided by storytelling. Before television and radio, and even before the printing press made books widely available, there was storytelling. Sitting around listening to the myths and legends

Children are very creative and require no outside stimulus when they have time to play. Here, for example, Chulupi Indian children find it amusing to stand on their hands.

STORIES OF THE MACÁ

Many indigenous stories, such as the stories of the Macá, try to explain origins or relationships. In their mythical stories, animals may behave like people. Here are two examples.

Origin of the Fish

Once a man lived alone with his son near a lagoon. All the women of their village collected water from a lagoon. The man told the boy to go to the path leading to the lagoon and wait for the women to pass. He was to call each woman "Mother" until one of them accepted him as her son. He did this and all the women ignored him except the last one. She took him home with her and raised him. He was given a bow and arrows when he was older and became a very skilled hunter. One day he was hunting in the forest and he lost an arrow. When he found it, it was stuck in a plant. When he pulled the arrow out, a big dorado fish jumped out of the hole. He brought the fish home to his mother and every day returned to the special plant for fish. The fox had been watching him secretly, and when the boy left one day, the fox started pulling out fish to eat. When he came to the biggest dorado of them all, it proved to be the master fish who ordered all the other fish to jump out of the plant bringing lots of water with them. The water carried the fish and fox into the rivers, and the fox had to turn into a gourd so he could float. That is how the fish got into the rivers.

How Jaguars and People Became Enemies

Jaguar, his wife, and their son lived near humans. He warned the human children not to come to his house and disturb his son. One day when Jaguar and his wife were out hunting, the children entered Jaguar's house and killed his son. Jaguar was so mad that he gathered all jaguars, entered the human village, and killed everyone. A man from another village saw vultures eating the dead people and decided to avenge their deaths. He built a very cunning house in the forest with a roof and only a small opening. Once inside, he started screaming so the jaguars would hear him. They did, and again Jaguar gathered his friends to get rid of the human. They circled the house but could find only one small window. As each jaguar entered, the man used his machete to cut off its head. One female jaguar escaped with her children. The remaining humans used the jaguar skins to make clothes and blankets. Since that time, people and jaguars have been mortal enemies.

of their culture was one way people learned their history and their religion. It functioned to bring the group together in a social setting and was and is a free form of entertainment.

Related to storytelling is the guarania or love song sung by a man to the woman he wishes to court. The man composes his own song to demonstrate the depth of his affection. Some guaranias have become popular, and people will also entertain themselves by singing and dancing to guaranias as a group.

FESTIVALS

PARAGUAYANS CELEBRATE both religious and historic holidays. Despite restrictions placed on the Catholic Church at various stages in Paraguay's history, people honor a number of Catholic festival days. Being very patriotic, they also celebrate quite a few anniversaries of important events.

DAY OF THE KINGS (EPIPHANY)

In the Catholic calendar Epiphany (January 6) is the day the Magi, or three kings, visited the baby Jesus and brought him gifts. Much of the religious significance of this day has faded in Paraguay. Just like Christmas in North America, Epiphany has become more secular.

Above: **Fiestas are for all organized groups, and schools participate by contributing their bands.**

Opposite: **Bullfights, a Spanish tradition, are the star attractions on festive days. This bullfight is in Yaguarón, about 25 miles (40 km) southeast of Asunción.**

In rural areas especially, people stage horseraces and other games on horseback. They also have archery contests and prizes are awarded to those possessing great skill with a bow and arrow. There may also be a competition to see who can climb a greased pole the fastest. This is hilarious for spectators and extremely difficult for contestants.

Tobatí, a small town east of Asunción, holds a religious procession accompanied by men in extravagant masks. They make the masks themselves in the form of animals or humans or a combination of the two. There are certain rules connected to this procession: they never use a mask more than once and they remain anonymous while wearing it. The men cover even their hands so no one can guess the identity of the person behind each mask. Self-preservation is the reason for this secrecy: the masked entertainers tell obscene jokes and tease people using false voices, offending many people by their antics. They accompany the religious procession but do not enter the church.

A religious festival is as much a time for public celebration as it is a time for religious faith.

SAINT BLAISE DAY

Saint Blaise is the patron saint of Paraguay and the saint of throats and throat afflictions. In one story, Saint Blaise was being led to his execution in A.D. 316 when he miraculously cured a child suffering from a sore throat. Since then sufferers of throat ailments have prayed to him.

Another story explains why he is the patron saint of Paraguay. In the early Spanish occupation of the place that would become Asunción, a fort was built to repel attacks from hostile Indians. On February 3, 1539, an apparition of a man in white on one of the fort's towers frightened away the Indian attackers. People believed that Saint Blaise appeared to rescue the Spaniards and proclaimed him the protector of Paraguay.

On February 3, processions are held in towns and in the countryside. The favorite attraction is a bullfight. The bull is decorated with paper streamers and flowers, and money is tied to its tail. The bullfighters do not try to kill the bull, they just try to get the money off the bull's tail without getting hurt, miming bullfighting techniques to entertain the crowds.

HOLY WEEK (EASTER)

This holiday commemorates Christ's crucifixion on Good Friday and resurrection on Easter Sunday. Like most Catholic countries, Paraguay celebrates Easter not just on two days, but for a whole week. During this time, there are religious processions through the streets and people attend Mass regularly. People do not work or go to school during Easter week.

In Paraguay, on the Saturday before Easter, people put on plays and processions about Judas, Christ's disciple who betrayed him to the Romans with a kiss. They build life-sized effigies of Judas and parade them through the streets. Then they stage a play in which "Judas" is tried and convicted for his crime of betrayal and a Judas effigy is hung or set on fire. In Paraguay, part of the fun is to fill the straw body of the effigy with firecrackers and then take turns shooting it with guns in an effort to set off the fireworks and make the effigy burn.

A CALENDAR OF FESTIVALS AND HOLIDAYS IN PARAGUAY

January 1	New Year's Day	June 12	Chaco Peace Day
January 6	Epiphany, Day of the Kings	June 24	Festival of Saint John
February 3	Saint Blaise Day, patron saint	June 29	Festival of Saint Peter
	of Paraguay	August 15	Founding of Asunción
February	Carnival (not as big as in	August 25	Constitution Day
	other Latin countries such as	September 29	Victory Day
	Brazil and Uruguay)	October 12	Day of Race (Columbus
March 1	Heroes' Day		Day)
March/April	Holy Week, Easter	December 8	Day of the Virgin of
May 1	Labor Day		Caacupé
May 15	Independence Day	December 25	Christmas

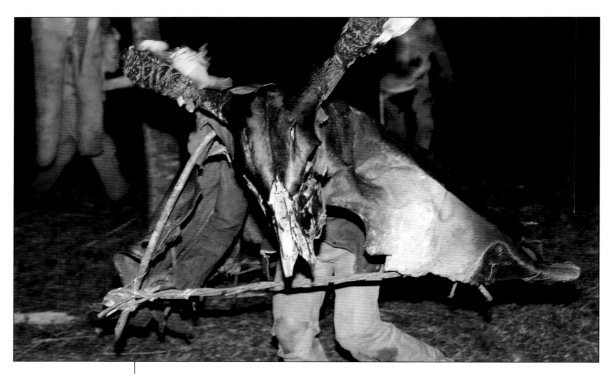

SAINT JOHN'S AND SAINT PETER'S DAYS

June 24 and 29 are dedicated to Saint John the Baptist and Saint Peter, respectively. Saint John's Day has long been associated with bonfires in Europe. When the Catholic Church tried to replace pre-Catholic midsummer celebrations with this religious observance, early beliefs in natural elements like fire were incorporated. On June 24 in Paraguay, celebrations begin with a special Mass in church.

The main spectacle of the festivities is the *toro candil* or candle bull. This is actually a man dressed as a bull with kerosene-soaked rags attached to a tail and horns. The bull chases people playing music and taunting him. At night this is quite a sight as the horns and tail are on fire. At some point, another character enters the arena: a child dressed as a rhea with a long stick for a neck and leaves for feathers. The child will also torment the bull by poking him from behind with the stick. A third character in this play is the *cheolo* ("chay-OH-loh"), a man who comes out of the crowd to challenge the bull. When all eyes are on the action, other men dressed as

Indians will charge into the crowds and start "kidnapping" women and girls. As they run off with the women, the remaining men will try to stop them. Young men in particular will try to bring back young women to their parents to show their masculinity. This play is so much fun for participants that they use Saint Peter's Day, five days later, to do it all over again!

Saint John's Day is also associated with superstitions. For example, rural women believe they must cut their hair on this day or it will stop growing the rest of the year. Young women wanting to know who they will marry write the names of potential mates on separate pieces of paper. They fold the pieces tightly and scatter them in the open, leaving them overnight. When they awake, the paper that has unfolded the most overnight reveals the name of their intended bridegroom. A darker superstition says that anyone who looks in a mirror in the middle of the night of June 24 and does not see his or her reflection will die the following year.

There are many local superstitions to do with divining future mates or death on Saint John's Day. The association of this day with marriage may go back to pagan days when people celebrated midsummer by pairing off at the end of the night.

THE VIRGIN OF CAACUPÉ

In the Catholic calendar, December 8 is the Day of Immaculate Conception, or the day the Virgin Mary conceived Jesus. The image of the Virgin at Caacupé is thought to have miraculous powers. The image was discovered by a Franciscan monk many years ago.

This is the most important religious festival in Paraguay, and everyone tries to participate. Those who can, will make a pilgrimage to Caacupé for the special Mass in honor of the Virgin. Many people who come suffer afflictions or carry sick relatives in the hope that the image of the Virgin will heal them. On this day Caacupé is converted into a town of festivities and attractions. Some Paraguayans bemoan the commercialism, saying they want it to be a purely religious celebration. Whenever lots of people gather, it seems even more are attracted in order to sell things.

The anthem of Paraguay was adopted in 1846 and starts with the words, "Paraguayans, Republic or death we choose!" Its composer is also responsible for the Uruguayan anthem. With so many countries gaining their independence and looking for songs to represent them, it must have been a booming business to write patriotic songs in those days!

During the 1960s, the Paraguayan Catholic Church made this day a political tool against Stroessner's dictatorship. The Mass was used to criticize Stroessner's abuse of human rights, and in 1969 the religious procession of the Virgin through the town was suspended as a protest against the regime. The suspension of the most cherished religious day of the year had some effect on Stroessner's popularity.

HISTORIC HOLIDAYS

Paraguayans are very patriotic and celebrate many historic days. Independence is celebrated on May 15 and commemorates the bloodless coup that gave Paraguay its freedom from Spanish and Argentinean control in 1811. This day is one of elaborate street parades in the capital

THE ONLY FLAG OF ITS KIND

Paraguay enjoys the distinction of having an unusual flag. What makes the flag stand apart is that its two sides are different. Both sides have three horizontal stripes: red, white, and blue. In the center of the white stripe is a charge (design). The charge on the front is the national symbol—a yellow five-pointed star surrounded by a wreath of palm and olive branches tied with a red, white, and blue ribbon. Within the wreath are the words *República de Paraguay* (Republic of Paraguay) in black. The charge on the back is the treasury seal—a yellow lion, a red cap of liberty, and the words *Paz y Justicia* (Peace and Justice) in blue.

The tricolor of red, white, and blue came to represent liberty, equality, and fraternity following the French Revolution in 1784. The French adopted these colors following the American Revolution of 1776. The two revolutions served as models for people seeking freedom all over the world, which is why you see so many flags using stripes in red, white, and blue. These colors originally came to America from the British flag called the Union Jack, which is also red, white, and blue.

A motorcade of police officers is part of the Independence Day parade in Asunción. The celebrations used to last two days, May 14–15, but that was changed in 1990.

city. People wear the national dress or the national colors of red, white, and blue. The national anthem is sung in the main square, and there are fireworks at night. Even the poorest will try to save enough money to afford the national dish (Paraguayan soup) on this day.

Constitution Day (August 25) celebrates the signing of the 1967 document. August 15 commemorates the founding of Asunción. Two days are dedicated to the Chaco War: June 12 and September 29. The first celebrates the signing of the peace treaty between Paraguay and Bolivia, while the second commemorates the Battle of Boquerón when the Paraguayans scored an important victory. Heroes' Day is for those who died in the War of the Triple Alliance: March 1 was when the final battle at Cerro Corá was lost and Solano López was killed. Other holidays observed in Paraguay are New Year's Day, Christmas, Labor Day (observed since 1906), and Day of Race (October 12), which commemorates the discovery of America by Christopher Columbus and indigenous peoples' contribution to Latin America. All of these days are usually observed as national holidays, though not all of them are legally designated as such.

FOOD

IN THIS FINAL CHAPTER, we will learn about important foods in the Paraguayan diet and how Guaraní culture has contributed to the national cuisine. Poverty is evident in the standard diet, as meat is considered a luxury.

TYPICAL FOOD AND PREPARATION

Paraguayan food differs from that of Argentina where meat predominates in the diet of even the rural poor. Meat is certainly important in the Paraguayan diet in regions where there is ranching, primarily the Chaco, but in the more populous eastern region, the standard diet derives more from the Guaraní heritage.

Above: **Bread piled high in a Caacupé street, in preparation for a feast.**

Opposite: **Corn is the main ingredient of numerous dishes in Paraguay.**

The two staple foods are corn and manioc, a root vegetable that can grow even in poor soils. Both staples are usually used as flour. Corn is dried, then ground using a wooden mortar and pestle. Manioc can be reduced to flour in two ways: soaked for a week in water or mud, then dried in the sun and ground; or sliced, dried, and then ground.

Dishes made with cornflour include *mazamorra* ("mah-zah-MOR-rah"), a corn mush; *mbaipy so-o* ("MBAY-pee SOH-oh"), a hot corn pudding with chunks of meat; *bori-bori* ("BOH-ree BOH-ree"), chicken soup with cornflour balls; and *mbaipy he-e* ("MBAY-pee AY-ay"), a dessert of corn, milk, and molasses.

From manioc, there is *mbeyu* ("MBEY-yoo"), a manioc-flour pancake grilled much like the Mexican tortilla; and *chipa* ("CHEE-pah"), a manioc bread with eggs, cheese, fat, anise, and milk. Chipa can also be served plain and usually is. Poor Paraguayans add eggs, cheese, and milk only for special occasions such as baptismal celebrations or national festivals. Manioc can also be eaten plain and boiled or roasted in coals.

Grilled meat is a typical Paraguayan fast food.

Soups are popular. *Soyo* ("SOH-yoh") is a meat and vegetable soup and *albóndigas* ("ahl-BOHN-dee-gahs") is a meatball soup. Fish appears frequently at meals. The most popular are two freshwater species native to Paraguayan rivers: surubí and dorado. For those who can afford it, there is also beef. The preferred method of cooking beef is on a barbecue called a *parillada* ("pah-reel-YAH-dah"), or grill.

The national dish is sopa Paraguaya or Paraguayan soup, which is not a soup at all but cornbread that includes onions and cheese. *Chipa guazu* ("CHEE-pah GWAH-zoo"), a lighter variation, resembles cheese soufflé.

Special foods are too expensive for daily meals. Sopa Paraguaya, for example, is not a staple food of the rural poor, but they will try to eat it on Independence Day or during religious or family celebrations. Meat is also expensive, so barbecues are reserved for days like Christmas. On Christmas, families often make a picnic out of the barbecue to make the day extra special.

Essential rural kitchen equipment includes the mortar for pounding corn and manioc and a metal grater for grating manioc. Sieves for sifting flour are made from finely woven reeds. Many people put food in green bamboo sections to bake or boil on an open fire. Gas is more readily available in the cities where people cook using gas stoves.

DRINKS

Apart from soft drinks and tropical fruit juices, Paraguayans enjoy *mosto* ("MOH-stoh"), or chilled sugarcane juice. As you can imagine, this is quite sweet. Other favorite beverages are made from the yerba maté plant. As

in Argentina and Uruguay, Paraguayans drink maté, a hot tea made from the leaves of this plant, which contain caffeine. During the hot summer months, they also make an iced version called *tereré* ("tay-ray-RAY"). Both are bitter. The main alcoholic drink is *caña* ("KAHN-yah"), a sugarcane alcohol produced locally. It is not unique to Paraguay since all sugarcane producing countries make it. Another alcoholic beverage popular here is *chicha* ("CHEE-chah"), which is made from fermented pineapple or corn.

Sunday dinner at home. Sunday is the day of rest for those with regular jobs, and families gather for the midday meal.

MEALTIMES

Mealtimes are adjusted for the summer heat. Paraguayans start the day quite early to avoid the wilting midday heat. Businesses typically open as early as 7 a.m. Then everything stops at noon, just when temperatures are rising. At this point there is a long break lasting three to four hours when everyone enjoys the main meal of the day. Since it is usually followed by a nap, people prefer to come home to eat. After siesta, they work until 7 or 8 p.m. People eat a light meal before going to bed. The day is also punctuated with lots of breaks to drink maté or tereré and socialize.

YERBA MATÉ

The yerba maté plant was discovered by Guaraní Indians who later taught the Spaniards how to drink maté tea. The scientific name for the plant, *Ilex paraguayensis*, reflects the fact that Paraguayans popularized it. The Guaraní did not drink maté as a regular beverage; for them, it was a medicine. Maté contains a number of vitamins, including A, B1, C, and niacin, and has been demonstrated to be good for headaches and muscle aches. It is also a stimulant like coffee and increases the heart rate. Once the Spaniards discovered it, they made maté drinking a part of their lifestyle. From there, it came to represent a particular aspect of Paraguayan society.

The traditional way to consume maté is from a special cup called a *guampa* ("gwahm-PAH"), made from a cow's horn. The leaves are packed into the cup and hot water is poured over them. To drink the liquid without getting a mouthful of wet leaves, one uses a *bombilla* ("bohm-BEEL-yah") or metal straw with mesh at the end to keep out the leaves. Ideally, one does not drink maté alone, but in company. Each person drinks from the cup, then refills it with hot water and passes it to the next person. The whole time, of course, people are chatting and passing the time away. The favorite time to enjoy maté is during the cool mornings. People do not necessarily go through the ritual of passing the cup except on special or formal occasions, but they still enjoy sharing each other's company over a cup of maté throughout the day.

Like maté, tereré has been part of Paraguayan life for a long time, but it is not associated with the same formalized ritual. As long ago as the 18th century, the Jesuits reported enjoying a cooler version of maté that they claimed alleviated both hunger and thirst. During the Chaco War, soldiers made tereré to cover the taste of the horribly muddy water they had to drink.

Both forms of the yerba maté plant are staple beverages and have played important roles in Paraguayan culture.

EATING OUT

Eating out is very much an urban phenomenon. Few rural people can afford to eat out, and besides, they do not have access to restaurants. In major centers, there are many snack shops selling various breads and puddings along with the ever-present maté and tereré. Street vendors move around the city or board buses and trains to sell food to travelers. They provide everything from hot, cooked food to cool, refreshing beverages. This is the way people eat when traveling in Paraguay.

Asunción boasts fancy restaurants. The typical formal restaurant is the parillada specializing in grilled meat served with boiled manioc. Such establishments may offer their guests entertainment, usually a musical ensemble featuring the Paraguayan harp and guitar, and sometimes even galopa or bottle dancers. Many Paraguayans never see the inside of a parillada restaurant because it is too expensive for them. For those who can afford it, a night out at a parillada is a social event.

In both Asunción and Ciudad del Este, there are quite a few Asian immigrants from Japan, China, and Korea. They have brought their cuisine with them, and now Paraguay is one of the best places in South America to find Asian food.

ALBÓNDIGAS: PARAGUAYAN MEATBALL SOUP

To make this delicious soup, you will need the following ingredients:

1 clove garlic, minced	1 cup soft breadcrumbs
3 onions, finely chopped	1 hardboiled egg, cut into small wedges
5 tablespoons cooking oil	2 cups tomato juice
2 pounds (1 kg) ground beef	2 whole tomatoes, chopped

Cook the garlic and two-thirds of the chopped onion in 2 tablespoons oil.

When the fried mixture is soft, mix it with the beef and breadcrumbs in a bowl.

Using your hands, make ping-pong sized balls out of this mixture. Place a small piece of egg in the center of each meatball.

Heat the remaining 3 tablespoons of oil in a frying pan and brown (lightly fry) the meatballs.

In a separate pot, simmer the tomato juice, the rest of the chopped onion, and chopped tomatoes until the mixture is thick. Add salt to taste.

Add meatballs to tomato sauce and simmer about 45 minutes, stirring occasionally.

When it is done, it makes about 8 servings of delicious and filling meatballs.

A   **B**   **C**   **D**

1

2

3

4

5

BOLIVIA

ALTO PARAGUAY

Gran Chaco

Chaco

Boreal

BOQUERÓN

BRAZIL

Paraguay

Menno

Fernheim

Filadelfia

Neuland

Pedro Juan
Caballero

Amambay Cordillera

CONCEPCIÓN

Concepción

AMAMBAY

PRESIDENTE HAYES

Tropic of Capricorn

Pilcomayo

Paraguay

San Pedro de
Ycuamandiyú

SAN PEDRO

CANINDEYÚ

Salto del
Guairá

Guairá
Falls

Oriental

Itaipú
Reservoir

Luque

CORDILLERA

Tobatí

Caacupé

CAAGUAZÚ

P a r a n á

ASUNCIÓN

Itauguá

Lake
Ypacaraí

Coronel
Oviedo

Ciudad
del Este

Itaipú Dam

CENTRAL

Lake Ypoá

GUAIRÁ

Villarrica

ALTO
PARANÁ

ARGENTINA

PARAGUARÍ

Numí

P l a t e a u

Lake Vera

CAAZAPÁ

San Rafael
Cordillera

Paraná

Tebicuary

Mount San
Rafael
(2,789 ft / 850 m)

ITAPÚA

N

Pilar

San Juan
Bautista

ÑEEMBUCÚ

MISIONES

Encarnación

Jesús

Trinidad

Yacyretá I.

Talavera I.

Paraná

PARAGUAY

Capital city

Major town

Mennonite
Communitie

Mountain p

Feet	M
16,500	5,
9,900	3,
6,600	2,
3,300	1,
1,650	5
660	2
0	

0	50	100 Miles
0	100	200 Kile

QUICK NOTES

OFFICIAL NAME
República de Paraguay, Republic of Paraguay

LAND AREA
157,047 square miles (406,752 square km)

POPULATION
5.6 million

CAPITAL
Asunción

PROVINCES
Alto Paraguay, Alto Paraná, Amambay, Asunción, Boquerón, Caaguazú, Caazapá, Canindeyú, Central, Concepción, Cordillera, Guairá, Itapúa, Misiones, Ñeembucú, Paraguari, Presidente Hayes, San Pedro

NATIONAL SYMBOL
A yellow star surrounded by the words República de Paraguay in black and a wreath of palm and olive branches tied with a red, white, and blue ribbon

NATIONAL FLAG
Three horizontal stripes of red, white, and blue; the white stripe has the national symbol on one side, and on the reverse, a lion and the words *Paz y Justicia* (Peace and Justice)

MAJOR RIVERS
Paraná, Paraguay, Pilcomayo

MAJOR LAKE
Itaipú Reservoir

NATIONAL LANGUAGES
Spanish and Guaraní

MAJOR RELIGIONS
Catholic, Mennonite, Native religions

CURRENCY
Guaraní (PYG)
US$1 = 2,835 guaranís (February 1998)

MAIN EXPORTS
Soybeans, cotton, textiles, wood products

MAIN IMPORTS
Machinery, cars, petroleum products

IMPORTANT ANNIVERSARIES
March 1—Heroes' Day
May 15—Independence Day
June 12—Chaco Peace Day (end of Chaco War)
September 29—Victory Day (Chaco War)

LEADERS IN POLITICS
José Gaspar Rodríguez de Francia—first president and dictator, 1814–40
Carlos Antonio López—dictator, 1841–62
Alfredo Stroessner—dictator, 1954–89
Juan Carlos Wasmosy—president, 1993–98
Raúl Alberto Cubas Grau—president, 1998–99
Luis Gonzalez Macchi—president, 1999–

LEADERS IN LITERATURE
Juan Silvano Godoi—art patron (1850–1926)
Josefina Plá—poet and sculptor (1909–)
Augusto Roa Bastos—novelist (1917–)
Gabriel Casaccia—novelist (1907–80)

IMPORTANT RELIGIOUS HOLIDAYS
January 6—Day of the Kings
February 3—Saint Blaise Day (patron saint)
March/April—Easter
December 8—Day of the Virgin of Caacupé

GLOSSARY

ahó poí ("ah-HOH POY")
A very fine handwoven cotton cloth.

bombilla ("bohm-BEEL-yah")
Straw used to drink maté.

caudillos ("cow-DEEL-yohs")
Political leaders who rule by threats and rewards.

code-switching
Changing from one language to another, a speech characteristic of bilingual speakers.

galopa ("gah-LOH-pah")
Women's folk dance in which bottles are balanced on the head.

guampa ("gwahm-PAH")
Cup made of cow's horn from which maté is drunk.

guarania ("gwar-ah-NEE-ah")
Paraguayan love-song.

guarañol ("gwar-ahn-YOHL")
A new language formed by combining Spanish and Guaraní.

Jesuits
Catholic priests who belong to a group called the Society of Jesus. In Latin America, they were missionaries in the colonial period.

maté ("mah-TAY")
Hot tea made from yerba maté leaves.

Mennonites
Protestants who believe in adult baptism.

mestizos ("may-STEE-sohs")
People of mixed Spanish and Indian descent.

monte ("MOHN-tay")
A type of vegetation in the Chaco region.

ñandú ("nyan-DOO")
Rhea, a large, ostrich-like bird.

ñandutí ("nyan-DOO-tee")
A cotton lace called "spider's web lace."

patrón ("pah-TRONE")
Large landowner, boss of peóns.

peón ("pay-OHN")
Peasant indebted to landowner or patrón.

poyví ("poy-VEE")
Coarse handwoven cotton cloth.

Reductions
Name given to Jesuit missions in South America.

shamans
Indigenous healers and priests.

syncretism
Blend of two or more sets of religious beliefs.

tereré ("tay-ray-RAY")
Cold drink made from yerba maté leaves.

yerba maté ("YAYR-bah mah-TAY")
Plant and herb used to make the tea, maté.

yopará ("yo-pah-RAH")
A jungle vine.

BIBLIOGRAPHY

Buckman, Robert T. *Latin America*. The World Today Series. Harpers Ferry, West Virginia: Stryker-Post Publications, 1997.

Childress, David Hatcher. *Lost Cities and Ancient Mysteries of South America*. Stelle, Illinois: Adventures Unlimited Press, 1986.

Fisher, John R. *Latin America: From Conquest to Independence*. London: Rupert Hart-Davis, 1971.

Haverstock, Nathan A. *Paraguay in Pictures*. Visual Geography Series. Minneapolis: Lerner Publications, 1987.

McNaspy, C.J. *Lost Cities of Paraguay: Art and Architecture of the Jesuit Reductions, 1607–1767*. Chicago: Loyola University Press, 1982.

Tames, Richard. *The Conquest of South America*. London: Methuen, 1974.

Wilbert, Johannes and Karin Simoneau. *Folk Literature of the Makka Indians*. Los Angeles: UCLA Latin American Center Publications, 1991.

INDEX

INDEX

INDEX

PICTURE CREDITS

Archive Photos/Reuters: 36, 79
Camera Press: 30 (top & bottom), 47, 94
Chip & Rosa Peterson: 1, 3, 4, 5, 18, 54,
   64, 78, 85, 98, 100, 117
DDB: 11, 16, 19, 33, 38, 46, 53, 60, 65,
   67, 69, 70, 80, 84, 93, 103, 108, 110,
   112, 115, 119
Victor Englebert: 12, 62, 92
Hutchison Library: 15
Björn Klingwall: 51, 99, 106
North Wind Picture Archives: 22
David Simson: 27, 44, 57, 72, 102
South American Pictures: 8, 13 (top &
   bottom), 17, 24, 25, 26, 39, 43, 50,
   55, 68, 76, 83, 86, 89, 90, 97, 104,
   109, 116, 118, 120, 123
Still Pictures: 40, 52, 61
Topham Picturepoint: 6, 7, 10, 20, 29,
   32, 42, 45, 49, 58, 74, 77